TEACHINGS

from

the

GATEKEEPER

*A Memoir and Journey
into Parapsychology*

DAVIS K. BRIMBERG, PhD

Praise for *Teachings from the Gatekeeper: A Memoir and Journey into Parapsychology*

"How refreshing to discover a book by a clinical psychologist that is so open and intimate, while simultaneously grounded in research! This book highlights the many paranormal events that punctuate the lives of more than half the population. It is a courageous book, both emotionally and scientifically. Sadly, most psychologists still maintain that paranormal phenomena do not merit their attention. Not so, Davis Brimberg. She understands that an appreciation of events ranging from precognition to after-death communication are fundamental to our human nature. I applaud this book and recommend it highly!"

— Jeffrey Mishlove, PhD, host and producer of *New Thinking Allowed* YouTube channel

"I wish I could give this book to everyone. It is a treasure chest full of fascinating parapsychological information and deeply moving personal stories. Richly researched and intelligent, Dr. Brimberg's writing offers invaluable insight and remarkable wisdom. I'm keeping this one in a permanent spot on my bookshelf and plan to refer to it again and again."

— Meaghan O'Leary, PhD, psychic medium and author of *A Medium's Memoir*

"Davis Brimberg is the ideal guide into the world of parapsychology. She lucidly discusses the best classical and contemporary parapsychological research as well as provides numerous absorbing accounts of her own and others' paranormal experiences, revealing how they can shake up our worldview and leave us profoundly changed."

— Roderick Main, PhD, professor and editor of *Jung on Synchronicity and the Paranormal*

For my beloved parents.

"Out of life's school of war:
What does not destroy me, makes me stronger."

—Friedrich Nietzsche
Twilight of the Idols (1889)

Contents

CHAPTER 1

The Bizarre Beginning: What Makes a Defining Moment?

IN 1991, A FEW MONTHS BEFORE MY EIGHTEENTH BIRTHDAY, I HAD a Defining Moment. As I write tonight, at the age of fifty, it is still the only one I have ever known.

On that day, I saw myself on a soul level. Typically, soul recognition is discussed within the context of two separate people connecting immediately and to a profound degree. Different writers on the topic explain that this experience happens when one person sees their "other half" in another individual. Yet, I did not see my other half in another person: I saw her within myself. Inside my Defining Moment lived an inherent duality. There was how I viewed myself prior to that day, and there was the permanent change in my self-perception after this one event. Never again would I understand myself in the same way. Although the facts of my life would remain intact, my interpretation of those facts and my perception of who I was were so greatly altered that it was as if a previous part of me had ceased to exist.

It all started on a sublime but brutal Saturday, in the winter of 1991. This one spiritual episode would forever change my life.

As a senior in high school, I had a big problem. Many years of academic struggles had left me so hopeless that I did not believe I could succeed at university. I did not even believe I could get in. My opinion did not matter to my parents. They demanded that I apply to a four-year college. They would not back down. Yet, I sensed that they did not believe I could pull it off. My parents' mixed-up doubts and hardline stance left me insecure and frightened. Never before had I felt such foreboding.

Desperately, I bargained. Since I did not believe I could get admitted to a decent school without dance, I told my parents that I would only attend university if I could do so as a dance major. They acquiesced: I had been taking dance classes, on their dime, since childhood; it was the one area where I showed promise. In truth, even at the time, I never believed I would become a professional dancer and choreographer. I just did not think I could do anything else.

While I had struggled academically as a child and teenager, I had also experienced, simultaneously, a remarkable awareness that my miserable trajectory would shift and my life would improve. This future self-knowledge was as clear to me as the brown eyes I saw every day in the mirror. Although largely comforting, it periodically made me feel "crazy," because my inner awareness did not match my external reality. I never mentioned this "awareness" to anyone; I believed others would think I was insane.

My belief that my life would improve and that I would, at some point, begin to succeed was more than just a coping mechanism; it was an unshakeable awareness gained only through intuition. Insights like mine come from within and are called *claircognizance*. While I never spoke to anyone about it, I clung on to this psychic, parapsychological insight as I would cling to a candle on the stormiest of nights.

Indeed, my claircognizance has guided me for as long as I can recall. And it would be with me, full tilt, on that arduous winter day.

Plea-bargaining with my parents to be able to major in dance also meant that I would face the daunting task of auditioning for college. All the most prestigious dance departments in the country required auditions, along with SAT scores and grades. I applied to four schools and, miserably, sent off to each my floundering academic records and my equally unimpressive test scores. As much as I wished, I could not hide my failures.

At the time, we lived in the suburbs of New York City, and on the day of my first audition, the tristate area was hit with a surprise blizzard.

My mother anxiously watched the news and grimly reported, "They've closed the highways."

We lived exactly one hour's drive away from the audition.

"All of them?" I asked, my eyes brimming.

"Yes. I cannot drive you into the city for the audition like we talked about. I'm sorry. They're closing the major roads. There's nothing I can do."

However, it seemed that the New York trains were still running, the Metropolitan Transit Authority apparently being apocalypse-proof. In the event of mass destruction, and also on this day of ill-timed inclement weather, it was still possible to take the Metro North train into Grand Central Station and then use the subway to reach the audition. It seemed so straightforward...but the plan had one terrible flaw: I, a teenager, had never navigated the MTA alone. My parents had forbidden it. (It is natural to wonder why a mother who was willing to drive into the city and back—an hour each way—would not be willing to ride a series of trains with her audition-bound daughter. But this logical question could only be raised by a person who had never met my mother.)

Seeing how distraught I was, my mother made a landmark exception: she said I could take the train into the city by myself. However, she then immediately countered that option with the statement that it would be "okay" if I chose to stay home instead.

"What?" I barked at her. Scrappy, resentful, fearful, I refused to accept defeat. But her discouragement combined with my own fears sent my sense of self plummeting.

Something inside her turned. Her face grew softer, her words more controlled. "Look, the weather is terrible," she said. "I'm concerned about your doing this. About your being on those trains alone. Walking around the city by yourself. I know your father would also be worried right now. Let's talk about your staying home."

As difficult as she could be, my mother made it clear to me that day, as she did every day, that she loved me. Underneath that profound love, though, lived her colossal fear of losing me. That morning, she was not focused on winning our battle. She wanted to protect me—whether from the weather or from an axe murderer sliding along the pavement in moon-walker snow boots, I'm not sure. Her powerful maternal instincts, strong as they were, came second to her fear of vulnerability.

My mother was in a state of inner conflict: Part of her wanted me to go into New York City and achieve my goal—she did tell me about the trains and the subway, after all. But a part of her also feared that her baby would get lost in the cold and fall prey to that axe murderer gliding along on the ice. She was a wreck; she was a Jewish mother; she was "born to worry."

As I heard the love and quake of terror in her voice, I was nonetheless offended by her suggestion that I stay home. Not so much because she was losing it on the day of my audition, but because it felt like just one more time my own mother did not believe I could accomplish something.

She was infuriating: her disbelief that I could manage the trains and successfully get in and out of Manhattan; her requirement that I go to college but then her telling me it was "okay" to miss the audition when we both knew it was not. So much of what she said was contradictory and further undercut my confidence. The audition was my only hope of getting into college, and college was the only choice my parents had given me. Her suggestion that I should stay home, accept defeat, and collude with the idea that I was an incapable person was toxic. All of it was insulting.

If I was stung by my mother's obvious fears, I was downright demolished by my father's continuing lack of faith in my intelligence. His opinion of me was at the epicenter of my pain. Each of us is wounded in our own way. My father's inability to see me as smart created, by far, my deepest wound.

Yet, in the middle of my indignation and teenage fury at my mother, my rational mind also knew she had a good point about the weather. It was bad outside. In the years to come, I would appreciate her wisdom. But on that day, the only thing I cared about was getting to the dance studio.

Once more, we argued. I changed into a leotard and tights, layered on some outerwear, and packed a bag of snacks. Right before I left the house, my mother sternly instructed: "Don't speak to anyone. If you get lost in the subways, ask a police officer or a transit worker for help. If you don't see one of them, ask a woman."

Three hours later, I stepped onto West 50th Street, the underworld of the subways and their winding tunnels behind me. All was quiet. There were very few cars or pedestrians in sight. Nor did I see a police officer, a transit worker, or a woman. The freshly fallen snow had blanketed the city, muffling what surrounding sounds were there. The city—normally teeming, vibrant, deafening, pregnant with possibility—was desolate, abandoned, almost post-apocalyptic in its immense silence.

My heart quickened as I trudged through snow piles toward 9th Avenue. When I reached the city's western limits, relief swept over me: I could see the studio up ahead and knew I would be arriving on time. I'd given myself three hours for a one-hour trip. But nothing had prepared me for what happened next.

Where is everyone?

The studio was enormous, an expanse made even more vast by the fact that it was totally empty. I stood in shock. I was the only dancer who had shown up. The room I was in, which was meant to hold a teeming group of aspirants, had a total population of four: the three evaluators...and me.

A short-haired woman with sparkly blue eyes told me how they had walked over from their hotel, which was just a few blocks away. She described the evaluators' national audition tour: two days in New York, one day in North Carolina, and two days in Illinois, after which they would head back to their California campus to see multiple rounds of in-state aspirants. Another woman, wearing bright red lipstick and her hair pulled back in a bun, asked how I had arrived. In a doomed effort to warm up my freezing body, I began to stretch. After more than thirty minutes of talking with me, they told me to take my place in the center of the floor. I immediately wanted to throw up.

Why did I do this?

Every bit of nervousness I had stowed away popped up. Up to that point, I had been so focused on simply getting to the studio that I had forgotten to be nervous about the audition.

The door suddenly looked appealing. Hurling myself headfirst through the windows and directly into the piles of snow didn't sound bad, either.

Really? After everything you've gone through? Really? You want to leave? You want to go home?

I felt numb, too scared to move. I started to space out and get dizzy. It wasn't even noon yet, and the day had already been a nonstop gut punch: the blizzard I could not have anticipated; the roads I could not clear; the showdown with my mother; the three labyrinthine branches of the MTA in which I sat, mute as ordered; the freakishly silent city; the slogging through snow and ice; the pressing terror of being late and possibly turned away. With a strength I didn't know I had, I breathed in deeply and somehow managed to move into the center of the studio. I wore only my leotard and tights. As is the case for all auditioning dancers, whose bodies are their first and only line of defense, there was one layer of Spandex in between me and my future.

It is a harsh, sad, and largely undiscussed fact that part of what dancers are judged on is their body. This is why they are not allowed to wear anything but a leotard and tights during formal evaluations. Every aspect of your weight, shape, and proportions is compared against a professional standard. Many girls are rejected by evaluators the moment they appear in dancewear. The talent of those trained dancers who have spent years diligently working in their local studios is deemed irrelevant. No one tells them this directly, of course. The beautiful dancers with the "wrong" bodies are simply cut alongside the less talented girls.

There is a basic way that auditions run and, by that point in my life, I knew how it was supposed to go: First, the dancers are assigned numbers and arranged at the barre by the evaluators. The audition that follows holds both ballet and modern technical portions. It starts with a ballet barre routine, and then everyone moves to the center of the studio. A ballet center combination is taught, with aspirants broken down into small groups. Once that segment ends, the modern portion of the evaluation starts. The dancers are paired up according to numerical order and are given modern choreography to perform diagonally across the length of the studio. Lastly, all the dancers come back to the center and are taught modern choreography to perform in small groups. Then, when everyone is good and sweaty, and maybe huffing for air, 85-90 percent of the dancers are removed by an evaluator announcing, "Would the following numbers please leave? I'm sorry. We're not interested." The remaining dancers perform their pre-choreographed solos and are then given their college interviews on the spot.

Inside that cold studio, with the evaluators settled comfortably into their chairs, snug in their overcoats, I stood in my leotard and tights alone in the middle of the floor, terrified.

In the center of the immense space, they showed me choreography and demanded, gently but with authority, that I perform it back immediately. There are no rehearsals at an audition. How well one learns and performs new choreography is assessed at once. They examined me, whispered among themselves, and scribbled notes on clipboards I would never read.

After what felt like an eternity, a second dancer arrived. Instead of seeing her as a competitor, I looked to this new dancer as if she were my oldest, dearest friend. No other dancers showed up.

As an adult, I can see now how fortunate I was to have had to audition during a weather disaster. Those evaluators would see people dancing at other auditions all around the country for weeks; but on that day, more so than they could have on any other day, they saw beyond my talents as a dancer: they saw my character, my courage, my determination, and my perseverance. And the evaluators were not the only ones to glimpse my inner self.

When I left the studio that day, I knew, for the first time in my young life, that I had accomplished something very difficult. Something that was deeply meaningful for me. I don't know what I did in the studio that day; I could not begin to show you the dance moves if I tried. But on that day—and for the rest of my days thereafter—I knew, and still know, that I did well. I hit the choreography as they wanted; but more than anything, when I exited the studio and trudged back once more through the snow piles towards the subway, I felt like a competent person.

That first, hard-earned, genuine success showed me that maybe, just maybe, I wasn't as much of a screwup as I had originally thought. Instead of seeing myself as someone who was doomed to fail, I saw a driven, goal-directed, efficient, competent girl who was so determined to achieve her objective that she arrived perfectly on time in the middle of a blizzard. Before this day, my belief that I was a failure was a sad but logical—and parentally reinforced—conclusion. I struggled so much in my academic subjects that when I was eight, I was given every psychological test imaginable; at seventeen, I was given all those same tests again. Neither professional examiner found anything wrong with me. But still I struggled. And my struggles extended well beyond academics. In gym class, I came in last. During the early years of dance, I could not coordinate the basic motions of a skip. I could not draw anything realistic in art class. Across nearly every category, my development was slower than and different from that of my peers.

But on this blizzard audition day, when Nature took down trees and power lines, knocked out roads, and brought JFK Airport to a standstill, I hit my own critical point. From the moment I left the audition, my childhood misery was behind me. What I saw ahead of me was the dawning of my new, successful adult life.

And my rebirth continued. Without any conscious awareness of my actions or their connection to my blizzard audition, I changed my name within a few months afterward. My doing so inspired ridicule from my community, but that was fine. The priority was that Karen, my given name, never really felt right; and now I had chosen something that did. I did not have a problem with the name itself, but I never identified with it. At the time, I could not verbalize why I did not see my original name as fitting.

Years later, when I made my name change legal, I told my parents separately by telephone. My mother cried. "You don't understand," she said. "I've loved you as Karen since before you were born, and now it's like that little girl is gone forever. I feel like she died."

I received a different response entirely from my father. He chuckled and said, "Well, you've somehow found a way to get reborn."

My Defining Moment held much duality. In it was a metaphorical death and rebirth. There was also a transition from failure to success and a passage from darkness to light. According to the theories of Carl Jung, MD, this one powerful event helped ignite a transformation within me in which I unconsciously integrated different parts of myself. It was through this synthesis of my different personality features that my life's course began to change.

I became more aligned with my Self that day, Jung would argue, because I was unconsciously ready to see who I had always been but somehow did not fully understand until that event.

The coming together of personality characteristics to form the Self was not unique to me. According to Jung, the never-ending formation of one's Self is shaped through a normal, unconscious, developmental process called Individuation.[1] Jung believed that people across every culture are called to go through Individuation. It is typically painful, but many people manage it and expand their sense of Self—becoming even more of who they are, psychologically. At the crux of what makes Individuation so difficult is the emotional task of figuring out who we are in relation to other people by more clearly understanding what matters most to us as individuals.

Individuation is a lifelong process, and it is not an all-or-none phenomenon. In some circumstances, a person is able to only partially navigate it. This can happen when a trauma (or another difficult life situation) interrupts someone's development. A person in this predicament develops only a partial sense of Self and lacks a solid internal compass. As adults, these people are vulnerable to the whims of others and are very often directionless. People with such poorly formed Selves are likely to have brittle and fragile self-esteems and chameleon-like tendencies, whereby they become whatever they believe another person wants.

Many people, thankfully, develop a stronger sense of Self through Individuation. They may never have a highly intense episode like a Defining Moment, but these moments are only extreme examples of self-discovery that exist within a context of many other self-realizing, developmental events.

Ironically, my Defining Moment blizzard audition was not even for my dream school. A week after that snowstorm audition, another was on the docket, and it was being held by my fantasy college: New York University's Tisch School for the Arts. Despite my new, stronger sense of Self, I knew my odds of my getting in were low. And while this statistical fact tested my claircognizance, my guiding, psychic awareness remained unchanged.

On the day of my audition for NYU, I was allowed to ride the train into Manhattan without question. As I traveled in, anticipating the difficulties in gaining admittance into my first-choice school, I thought, *You won't be alone. The weather's fine. Just enjoy it.*

This time, the audition space was packed. Forty of us sweaty girls (and a couple of boys) battled it out in a gigantic studio. Our leotards were pinned with numbers before we lined up at the barre. Just before we began, we were reminded that anyone who left the studio during the audition, for any reason, would forfeit their chance of admittance. Then the four evaluators, clipboards in hand, took up their positions in each of the studio's four corners.

They pumped the music. Every move we made was observed. Noted. Clipboarded. This studio was a tank filled with sweat, ambition, and fear. Twenty minutes into it, not even halfway through, one girl ran out in tears. I wondered what happened to her. Did she miss a step? Did she even grab her bag? I couldn't look.

Once we finished the final section, the quartet of evaluators huddled in hushed conference and compared their clipboards. Minutes passed; we held our breaths. Eventually, one of them, a tall, leggy blonde, emerged, staring dead-eyed into the middle distance:

"Would the following numbers please leave? I'm sorry. We're not interested. Thank you for coming out today."

I couldn't look at her. Staring at my swollen feet, I listened to her femmebot, disembodied flat voice call out numbers in an asynchronous, torturous random order.

"Twelve, thirty-five, two, forty..."

Cue the pleading phase in my head: *Please, God. Please don't let this woman say Number Three.*

"Twenty-eight, seventeen, thirty-one, nine..."

She was a fearsome femme-bot, but there was no malice in her—just complete indifference to our admission to the program. Something many of us had worked for years to get into.

Cue the bargaining phase: *Please, God. I can do better. I'll do everything right for the rest of my life; just don't let her say my number.*

The femme-bot did not mention Number Three.

Breaths released. From forty, we were now five. My relief had barely kicked in when it was replaced with a hit of adrenaline: next up was a solo. Mine.

The second portion of the day's audition remained, and it was the hardest part. Many barriers had been crossed, but Number Three was still nowhere near her goal.

Ultimately, I was accepted into both the blizzard audition school and New York University. The news from NYU arrived in a strange way: I received two different letters from the same school, on the same day. One was a rejection letter from the general university, and the other was an acceptance letter from the dance department. The dance department wanted me badly enough that they overrode the general university's rejection and forced the school to take me.

With this acceptance, I glimpsed a possible new life for myself. It was only a hint. A flash. But it seemed within reach.

During the first month of college, terrible and beautiful things began to happen. Each of them strangely foreshadowed what was to become my life's work. Indeed, the initial days of NYU were striking harbingers of the psychologist's journey I would eventually undertake.

Maybe the sadists who ran the dance department organized the semester as they did for the simple love of torture. Freshmen and sophomores were mixed together and placed into different sections based on how well or how poorly each performed, which effectively forced us to re-audition against each other on a daily basis for two weeks.

Each of us had been one of the strongest dancers at our home studios, and each of us now felt like the worst dancer on the NYU campus. During our first weeks of college, away from our parents for the first time—as if settling into dorm rooms was not stressful enough—we were getting to see exactly how much talent existed outside of our hometown bubbles.

The amount of talent I was surrounded by was staggering. Demoralizing. One girl was so extraordinary that I seriously could not figure out how I got into the same school she did. That immediate and disturbing dose of reality left me convinced that I could be kicked out of the program. Somewhere around day four, I decided that if I could just make it through to the end of week two, the department might allow me to stay.

Oddly, in the middle of week two, three of my freshmen dance classmates came to my dorm room—separately, and unannounced—in different states of distress. I was surprised to see them, since we were still strangers. Although countless friends had confided in me during my childhood and teenage years, these new people did not know me. We had only been together for a short period, and most of our class time was spent not talking, but simply trying to survive as instructors scolded, "What's going on? The right leg extends on the floor quickly on Two! Then, you drag the leg back in, slowly into the body. Why is that not happening today? It's a musical cue, people! Let's do it again."

And yet, three dancers from my cohort knocked on my door, each one asking to talk. We were not friends yet, but somehow they knew I would hold their secrets and fears. Inside my dorm room, they told me their worries. They spoke longingly of home. And although they never directly stated it, I could hear them mourning for the days of feeling like the best. NYU's daily bouts of re-auditions had dismantled and shredded their egos. One of them was a girl named Carla, from Austin, Texas. "Sometimes, I'm not sure whether I should be here," she confided. "Things feel off. I'm not totally myself. I don't know if I can last."

I listened to Carla and the others with great empathy. I allowed them to talk, to get everything out. I chimed in where appropriate and intuitively knew to keep the conversations to myself. I never told anyone that they had come to see me. I did not realize at the time that, on those nights after class, I wasn't just listening to potential new friends; I was providing counseling to distraught strangers.

Somehow, in our time in the dance department during rare, brief conversations, they had sensed that they could trust me. Looking back, I suspect that what they picked up on were my empathy and my innate understanding that what they told me was not to be shared. I was thankful and flattered that they confided in me. During those late-night discussions, I also saw that my listening and empathy made a difference in their lives. I was glad to be able to help them.

Soon thereafter, I started weekly psychotherapy sessions with a very talented psychiatrist. The pain from so many years of academic failure was so sharp that it had left me depressed. As a psychotherapy client, I saw that I needed to call upon a willingness—and an ability—to self-reflect.

While I spent many hours in tears on my psychiatrist's couch (and for years thereafter), my time in therapy allowed me to piece together the sources of my academic problems. Our work together was an intense and profound excavation that pulled out answers from the ruins and debris of my psyche.

The process of examining my unconscious, wherein we discussed my dreams, family dynamics, and relationships, was both helpful and fascinating to me. Through my sessions, I saw how leaving one's unconscious unexamined could create blocks and hurdles that could severely damage that person's life—and how, if that person understood themselves more, they could feel empowered to change their life for the better. Within months, I found myself more comfortable exploring the unconscious in a psychiatry office than I had ever felt dancing in a studio.

As my psychotherapy progressed, other bizarre things that foreshadowed who I would become as an adult began to occur. I started to perform well academically. This was not a miracle that transpired over the course of a single class. Strong grades sprouted up in all my academic classes: Literature, Women's Studies, and…Introduction to Psychology.

While I blossomed academically, I realized that, despite the promise I'd shown in getting accepted to college, I would never have a career in dance. Although I was not the worst in my classes, I was nowhere near the top; and I knew the professional dance world was filled with girls even more talented than many of my most gifted classmates. These were all blatant facts that I could not ignore.

Remarkably, I felt relieved by my decision to leave dance. I no longer felt trapped by the idea that I could do nothing else. Finding myself thriving in the world of academics was exciting. My transformation may have begun on the day of my Defining Moment, during my blizzard dance audition, but dance was merely the catalyst that would lead me toward soul recognition.

My Defining Moment had launched a shift in my self-perception that was great enough to get me admitted into NYU—the only college I applied for that was connected to a major university, and the only school that could possibly have sent me down a true academic path. (The other schools I auditioned for were conservatories.) The dancers who knocked on the door of my dorm room, strangers at the time, were, in a bizarre way, forecasting my client sessions. NYU was the only school I applied for that was in Manhattan, the city where my treasured psychiatrist would both help and inspire me to see the world through a clearer, richer lens.

After my freshman year, I left the dance department to become a psychology major, growing steadily into an A student. In the end, I graduated with honors from the same college that had initially rejected me. The very university that only admitted me because I could dance watched me turn into one of their top academic performers. Years prior, as a high school senior, I had frantically tried to avoid college due to my fear that I would never graduate. How wonderful it was to have been so very wrong.

My sister told me our father cried during my college graduation. In my lifetime, I only saw him cry twice: once at his mother's funeral, and then again, about a decade later, while we were observing a group of strangers. On that day, my parents and I saw several teenage ice skaters training with their coaches at an ice rink. The girl closest to us struggled with a spin-and-jump combination. Each time she tried the routine, she fell on the ice, got herself back up, and tried again. After her fifth or sixth attempt, my father openly wept and said, "It's beautiful."

I was stunned by his reaction to the girl—a skating, stumbling symbol of my childhood.

After my college graduation, I continued to receive A's and academic honors as a Master's and PhD student. My graduate studies were both exciting and reassuring. I felt inspired by the books we studied and comfortable in my classes. I taught my first semester-length college course at the age of twenty-six.

Did I foresee the abundance of possibilities—wondrous career paths—that I would have before me? Throughout my youth, my claircognizance had told me my pain would end, but it did not tell me that one defining, spiritual episode would set off my self-discovery and ultimately position me for my life's calling.

A person in a Defining Moment, often triggered by adversity, suddenly finds themselves stuck in a challenging, unforeseen circumstance that they must navigate. They respond by deeply listening to themselves, perhaps more than they ever have before. Then they take some action that unabashedly honors their individual spirit. The action taken at a Defining Moment is supremely aligned with that individual's sense of rightness.

On the surface, it appears a Defining Moment is only about the person who actually experiences it. But as I have delved deeper into this topic, I have seen a consistent theme across Defining Moments: These rare events all seem to result in the betterment of other people. This theme is so clear to me, so apparent, that I now believe the purpose of Defining Moments is for the collective—not simply for the individual.

This was certainly true of my Defining Moment. Not only did it profoundly change my sense of Self; it also set me on a path to help others. By the time I turned fifty years old, I had helped hundreds of clients through many thousands of hours of counseling. As a college professor, I have taught hundreds of undergraduate and graduate students, many of whom have gone on to become psychologists and help hundreds of clients themselves.

There are many beautiful examples of Defining Moments that benefit far more people than just the individual. Qamar is a client of mine who had a Defining Moment at nineteen years old when he made the decision to give away his entire college scholarship (consisting of one full year's tuition) to a needy classmate. He made this gift as a college sophomore, ninety days after his father had suffered a fatal heart attack in front of him.

Another teenager with a Defining Moment is David McGillivray, who longed to be a professional athlete but was too small. Consistently cut during team tryouts, and always the other children's "last pick" for athletic games, McGillivray nevertheless decided to run the Boston Marathon at the age of seventeen. That day, he was unable to finish the race and ended up in the hospital.

The following year, on marathon day, McGillivray's worried parents tried to stop him from racing, but he insisted that he was going to finish it this time and begged to be given a chance. Midway through the race, he began to struggle and seriously question whether he could continue. He contemplated quitting but instead got up and started running again. He finished that race and has run it every year since the 1970s. Eventually, McGillivray became the director of the Boston Marathon, and he has helped organize more than 1,400 mass athletic events while raising millions of dollars for charities.[2] Every year, McGillivray runs the marathon in Boston, and while it begins at 10 a.m., he starts at 8 p.m. to ensure he finishes in last place.

Even more powerful Defining Moment stories have arisen throughout history. Consider how much better our society became when Rosa Parks refused to give up her bus seat for a White passenger in 1955. Consider, too, the day when Winston Churchill escaped a prisoner-of-war camp as a young man and how that day would foreshadow his courage to lead England as Prime Minister during the country's "darkest hour." Think of Mahatma Gandhi, who, after being forcibly thrown off a train in his youth due to the color of his skin, vowed to defend Indian rights. All Defining Moments, famous or not, boil down to the same theme: serving the collective, in addition to the individual.

Another common thread the reader may have noticed is that most Defining Moments happen during adolescence and young adulthood. (Parks is an exception. She was forty-two.) Jungian theory suggests that this is not a coincidence. This age bracket perfectly aligns with the height of the Individuation process.

Doctor Sigmund Freud, the founder of Psychoanalysis, and Jung's greatest influence, would see sublimation built inside the dynamics of Defining Moments. Freud first conceptualized this psychological defense mechanism in 1910 and explained how sublimation occurs when a person unconsciously takes their innate impulses, such as anger, and transforms that same energy into some socially acceptable form.[3] My anger toward my mother and, by extension, my father, on my blizzard audition day helped propel me out of the house and get me on that train for Manhattan.

Defining Moments are typically born from anger and emotional pain. The humiliation Gandhi suffered during the train incident, for example, set off his lifelong promise to protect Indian people. Was Gandhi also angry as he sat alone inside that cold, dark train station? Could Rosa Parks have been resentful of all the racism she had suffered before getting on the bus that day? How did Churchill feel while trapped inside a prisoner-of-war camp? Was my client Qamar angry when he suddenly lost his father at the age of nineteen? Was McGillivary angry that he was born too small for professional sports and consistently the "last pick" in the schoolyard? How could I not have been angry with my parents for not seeing me as smart? Defining Moments often start with someone enraged about something. In each circumstance, a person transforms their anger into some action that eventually serves other people.

Nestled beside the anger within Defining Moments is defiance. Defining Moments are fundamentally acts of disobedience. They are rebellions. Uprisings of One. They begin with an individual resisting expectations from parents (and other emotionally significant figures), expectations from themselves, expectations from institutions, from society. Crushing or actively denying those expectations, an individual's Defining Moment is a time of extreme authenticity in which they establish their commitment to their individual spirit. My client, Qamar, for instance, had earned his scholarship for his academic accomplishments. It is blatantly against the rules for one student to hand a scholarship to another student; it's so unthinkable that most scholarship guidelines don't even address the possibility of it.

Nevertheless, Qamar honored what "felt right" to him—to give the needier student the money, despite the university's policies.

Beneath the anger and defiance is also self-love—perhaps the most crucial ingredient in these rebellions. Even in the most horrible of times, even within the deepest sector of one's misery, a person with a Defining Moment has enough self-regard to launch themselves into their transformation to become their true Self. No one can listen that closely to themselves, refuse to accept some unacceptable status quo, and take corrective action without loving themselves in some way, no matter how deep down that love resides.

Each of us, with our respective Defining Moments, was trapped, physically or emotionally or metaphorically, by our circumstances. All of us were Underdogs. Outsiders. Fighters. As a boy, Churchill landed in the bottom of his class for years at his fancy boarding school.[4] During her childhood, Parks was repeatedly bullied by the White kids in the neighborhood.[5] And although I have never affected—and will never affect—society the ways these extraordinary folks did, I sure was pissed, and I sure was determined to break free from the confines of my status quo.

Just as we are programmed to keep breathing on a battlefield, we have within us a constant need to Individuate. This soul-based drive, this outright demand to develop one's true Self, becomes unstoppable during the Defining Moment—that special, mysterious event whereby people and systems are defied, while another Self flowers into existence and serves the collective good.

My Individuation hit a peak on the day of my Defining Moment, but the process of me becoming more of my true Self did not start on that Saturday. As with all of us, my journey to becoming a distinct individual began much earlier in childhood. In retrospect, I see how much my claircognizance steered my separation and emotional development.

From its "heightened intuition," my claircognizance guided me to become who I was meant to be. My claircognizance knew my years of struggle would end, and because of this understanding, I progressed forward and eventually transformed. I did not simply continue to try whenever I failed only because I was tenacious. I continued my efforts, in the face of failure, largely because I already knew the bottom line: life for me would improve.

Yet my claircognizance about my general path was only one of many psychic experiences that I had as a child. The academic difficulties I dealt with were partly due to my being distracted by the psychic and emotional information around me. For example, it would not be unusual for me to wonder during an algebra lesson, "Why is Mrs. Adams still upset about the fight she had with her husband last night?"

Over the course of my life, I have experienced a few hundred psychic episodes. While this is a sizeable amount of intuitive "hits," this number is nothing compared to a professional psychic, who by my age will typically have had thousands of these incidents. Thus, I may be more psychic than the average person, but I am far less psychic than a professional. Nevertheless, my psychic abilities are natural parts of who I am. Today, whenever I feel a heightened sense of intuition, I listen carefully and with an open mind to whatever it is I am feeling. I am intrigued and curious, and I trust that if my intuition is sensing something, it is for my benefit.

But in the beginning, I did not always find solace in my psychic abilities. I often thought I was strange or weird. How did I know what was upsetting Mrs. Adams? Did the other children know she had fought with her husband the night before? These episodes confused me. Complicating it all was the fact that I grew up in a family that did not welcome discussions on the paranormal or spirituality. Because the topics were viewed as illogical, I kept my questions and, most of all, my experiences to myself. Even into my adulthood, I told only a few close friends about my psychic experiences.

My efforts to hide the way I was wired or even shut down my parapsychological abilities were futile, though. I could not deny the existence of the paranormal to myself, and I could not ignore my awareness of another realm that extends beyond our physical plane.

Now, more than ever, as an adult and as a psychologist, I have come to embrace this very natural side of myself. My intuitive abilities are parts of me, just as my height and white skin are some of my innate physical features. One of the beautiful things about turning fifty is that you care less than you ever have about how others see you. But that was not always the case, of course. Before I arrived at this point in my life, before I ventured off on a scholarly discovery of the paranormal and parapsychology, I simply wanted to understand why a subject so real to me could be so strange and unbelievable to other people. As I delved deeper into the material and investigated the topic more, I found that reputable, scholarly information appeared most often in separate academic books and journals. Very few works of this nature had synthesized the highly regarded material into one book, and those that had done so failed to present the research in a fun, accessible way. For readers who feel the same, this book is for you.

This book is for anyone who has been curious about what scholars have discovered about the paranormal. Similarly, it is for those who have wished their university provided a course in parapsychology. And, this book is for anyone who has ever heard, felt, or seen Spirit, shared those experiences, and were told by their listener that whatever they reported must not have been real. My book is for readers who have felt shut down, invalidated, and perhaps even ostracized by others who did not share the perspective that there may be another dimension outside of our immediate, physical boundaries.

And to my delight, the more I read about this subject, the more I discover about how the paranormal has been studied by some of the greatest minds of all times.

My interest in the paranormal originated from my own psychic experiences and developed from my need to honor my true Self. Throughout my adulthood and my career as a clinical psychologist, my interest in and understanding of parapsychology has remained—and even grown. It is an area of passion and fascination that has, over time, brought me great comfort.

To me, as a psychologist, the tendency for my field to disregard parapsychology is baffling. Psychologists study the ways in which people behave, think, and attach to one another. They seek to understand the subtleties within human behaviors, such as how our developmental histories affect our personalities. Parapsychological episodes reveal our humanness—just as they reveal the possibility of another realm. Within paranormal incidents, we see the cognitive, social, and emotional nuances in which we function as people.

Despite the obvious parallels between psychology and parapsychology, most universities in the United States do not offer classes in parapsychology, a telling sign of how this specialty area has been dismissed. And, of course, the psychology department leaders who compose their curricula are not alone in omitting this material.

Readers do not need to travel far to find invalidating voices on parapsychology. They're often seated around a family dinner table or living down the hall. The world is filled with naysayers who do not know the facts but still feel comfortable disparaging parapsychological phenomena. In this book, I will not present the specifics of the naysayers' arguments. I will discuss the critics' general positions, though, wherever necessary, since it is important to understand the concepts they are objecting against. As Jung explains,

> *People deny the findings of parapsychology outright, either for philosophical reasons or from intellectual laziness. This can hardly be considered a scientifically responsible attitude, even though it is a popular way out of a quite extraordinary intellectual difficulty.*[6]

It is my greatest wish that we examine this controversial subject from the perspective of strong academic study. Thankfully, over the years and throughout my research for this book, I have found a wealth of high-level scholarship on the topic. I believe the best way to address these denigrating perspectives is through close, professional, academic study.

The naysayers' voices are loud. In this book, I counter their arguments with solid research. I have brought high-level studies into these controversial conversations because parapsychology deserves to be fully and properly examined. Psychic phenomena are natural variations of human behavior that have existed for thousands of years; they will persist for as long as humanity remains, regardless of anyone's denials, distortions, or protests.

So, let us push aside the pressures and biases of society and step forward into this fascinating and timeless subject.

As they say in dance studios across the world, "Let's start from the beginning: 5,6,7,8."

A NOTE TO THE READER

THE READER MAY WONDER HOW I CAME TO DECIDE WHICH TOPICS TO include in this book, given the enormity of the field of parapsychology. In choosing my topics, I felt it was necessary for there to be a strong overlap between something I had personally experienced and the high quality of the academic material available (an exception is the chapter on near-death experiences, which I have never had).

I curated the book in this manner so that I could share my experiences as teaching examples and then use them to help explain case studies, famous stories, and research findings. Interestingly, although the vast majority of colleges do not offer courses in parapsychology, some of the finest schools in our country do have researchers exploring the paranormal, and it is these professionals' work that I have included for the reader. Most of the research I will present here comes from major academic institutions, including the University of Virginia, Yale, and Cornell. The studies and results I cite come from researchers, professors, *professors emeriti*, and Nobel laureates. Much of the research I cover has been published in peer-reviewed journals, textbooks, and other scholarly books. The theorists whose work fills many of these pages are Carl Jung, Sigmund Freud, Albert Einstein, and Wolfgang Pauli.

CHAPTER 2

The Building Blocks

AFTER FINISHING GRADUATE SCHOOL AND MY POSTDOCTORAL TRAIN-ing, I moved out West and started my career in Los Angeles. Professionally, I divided my time between seeing clients in my private practice and teaching college students. It was an exciting and special period layered with uncertainty and optimism. In my downtime, I read about parapsychology, not knowing I would one day write this book.

Although I had read some of Carl Jung's works in school, I decided to study his theories in greater depth. My rationale was simple: No single theorist has contributed more to the field of parapsychology than Jung. For this reason, I will reference him often.

But before I present Jung's bountiful and inspiring work in more detail, we must first review several terms and concepts critical to parapsychology. They represent the building blocks and scaffolds for this specialty area.

Frequently Asked Questions

How are the words paranormal *and* parapsychology *different?*

Paranormal events disrupt our understanding of time and space. Parapsychology examines how paranormal phenomena are perceived. For example, let's imagine seeing a ghost. The ghost's presence is a paranormal event, whereas the experience of seeing that ghost is parapsychological.

Parapsychology is often defined as the study of experiences that are beyond the realm of human capabilities as conventionally believed by science.[1] Researchers within this field study psychic phenomena that are generally referred to as psi. Although the little word "psi" may seem like an acronym, it is not.

What is psi?

Psi includes a large category of intuitive abilities not readily explainable by our five standard senses. Such intuitive Extrasensory Perception, or ESP, includes the following.

- Clairaudience: extrasensory perception gained from hearing psychic messages

- Claircognizance: extrasensory knowledge gained only by intuition

- Clairsentience: extrasensory awareness solely through feeling

- Clairvoyance: extrasensory knowledge of events, people and objects at various points along the future

- Mediumship: also known as channeling; the ability to communicate with spirits

- Near-Death Experience: involves a transcendental experience from a direct confrontation with death[2]

- Precognition: extrasensory knowledge of a future event

- Premonition: a general forewarning; a vague extrasensory feeling that something ominous will occur

- Reincarnation: The notion that after death, a person or an animal's soul can be reborn into another physical body

- Retrocognition: extrasensory awareness of a past occurrence

- Synchronicity: an event in the outside world coincides meaningfully with one's psychological state[3]

- Telepathy: mind-to-mind communication; the ability to send and receive thoughts

What is the occult?

The occult is a large category that consists of both supernatural beliefs and parapsychology. Spirituality, astrology, magic spells, tarot cards, and the various ESP abilities, for instance, are all different aspects of the occult.

What is the difference between a psychic and a psychic medium?

A professional psychic uses multiple psi abilities to understand people, situations, or objects, while a psychic medium has the additional ability to communicate with the dead. Both may use tools such as tarot cards to help guide their process, but only psychic mediums are capable of channeling spirits. This ability involves receiving messages from spirits, as well as relaying those messages to people affected by the deceased.

Psychics and psychic mediums have been known to work with the police to help solve crimes. Typically, when psychics do this work, the skill they rely upon is retrocognition. In most cases, they are given an article of clothing or a photograph of the victim, or they visit the victim's home or the actual crime scene.[4] So far, I have not learned of any cases in which a psychic or psychic medium has served as an expert witness in a criminal court.

When do parapsychological abilities develop?

Most people with psychic abilities show signs in childhood. A team of researchers in 2017 found that 81 percent of psychic mediums had their first experience during childhood.[5] People without psychic tendencies, however, may have isolated parapsychological experiences in their lifetime.

A skeptic friend of mine recently confided that she "never believed in anything spiritual" until she encountered "weird experiences" around the time of her father's death. For a few weeks after his passing, my friend repeatedly sensed her deceased father's spirit inside her bedroom. She was shocked and eventually concluded that "something spiritual must have happened." As a result of her direct experiences, this once-devout skeptic began to soften on the subject. She found these episodes "too real" to disregard.

Early parapsychological researchers first noted how psi experiences tended to increase during intense and emotionally heightened periods,[6] such as after a loved one's passing. Many other researchers since have confirmed this observation.

Who gets to have psychic abilities, and why?

At the core of all psychic abilities is intuition, something we are all born with. This is why each of us, even devout skeptics like my friend, have the potential for psychic phenomena. Similarly, highly empathic people tend to be more intuitive, and therefore more likely to have psychic abilities. Keep in mind, however, that a person can be highly empathic and hold very little or zero psychic tendencies. The abundance of empathy only sets one up for *potential* psychic abilities.

Some people seem to be born with more intuition than others, but this skill can be strengthened with practice, just like anything else. Consider running, for instance. Anyone born with a standard, able body can learn to run—I know toddlers who pretty much do nothing else. There are, of course, people who are more naturally athletic; but everyone, regardless of baseline talent, can become a better, more efficient runner with training and motivation. Conceptually, intuitive abilities are no different. Professional psychics may start out with greater natural intuition, but they practice and strengthen their innate abilities over time.

We hear many people use the word "gifts" to describe psychic abilities. Intuition is natural and essential, and therefore not inherently unique or special. In my opinion, the word "gifted" is more appropriate for psychic mediums. The ability to both channel and communicate with spirits is rarer than general psychic abilities.

Nevertheless, all of us are biologically wired for intuition; this function serves an important evolutionary role. Intuition safeguards our survival and helps ensure the survival of our offspring. Consider how often our cavemen ancestors needed to sense something dangerous was headed their way. Intuition was the only thing these very early people had to aid their survival!

Such an adaptive conceptualization of psychic ability further explains why people often have their first—and only—psi experiences during extreme situations. My friend's awareness of her deceased father's spirit is a good example of how an emotionally difficult situation set off a series of psi phenomena. In particular, we see that my friend experienced *clairsentience* for the first time.

The idea that psi stems from intuition is supported even more by the fact that researchers see a paucity of parapsychological phenomena during mundane circumstances. Banal, everyday experiences do not set off internal, intuitive alarms that something important needs attention. For example, a psychically oriented person probably would not see that they were about to get into a traffic jam, if getting stuck on that highway for an extra twenty minutes would have no significant impact on their life.

Psi experiences are both psychologically normal and helpful. I can confidently report that nearly all my psi events guided me for the better in some way. Overwhelmingly, what I have seen is that my intuitive moments prepared me for difficult circumstances. This was especially true when it concerned the well-being of loved ones.

Is it true that psi "runs in families"?

When considering the origins of psi, many people have argued that para-psychological abilities "run in families." While biology may be a factor, I have not seen any definitive genetic studies that conclusively prove the heritability of psi. Nothing indicates that psi capacities are truly genetic traits such as eye color.

In 2022, researchers looked for genetic markers of psychic abilities and found no conclusive evidence.[7] Similarly, another team of researchers in 2018 examined a sample of 3,023 adults and found that 53 percent of psychic mediums had family members with "similar experiences."[8] This number is especially interesting when we consider that mediums are often believed to be the most psychically oriented people. Although a percentage of 53 percent is considerable, it is not high enough to prove that psi "runs in families." Overall, genetics may play an important role, but the extent of biological influence on psi remains unclear. More than likely, it is the combination of biological and environmental factors that best explains the presence of shared psi abilities among family members.

Which environmental factors increase the likelihood that multiple family members will have psychic abilities?

Certain environmental factors may increase the possibility of psi among family members:

A PARENTAL BELIEF IN THE PARANORMAL

Being raised in a family, and/or a community, that is open to paranormal topics is a large environmental factor that can exert a powerful effect on a developing person. Such a spiritually minded environment could strongly impact how paranormal events are both experienced and interpreted.

THE IMPACT OF TRAUMA

Trauma is another environmental factor that may greatly affect psi abilities that may also be shared among family members. But how does trauma play a role in psi, exactly?

People with histories of abuse and neglect often develop hypervigilance; they unconsciously scan their environments, in mundane situations and extreme ones, for potential emotional and physical threats. This heightened emotional state causes a person to remain on high alert, which may magnify someone's intuition. Unfortunately, heightened emotional states may also cause people to misread cues, even to the point of paranoia.

Hypervigilance can also occur in children who regularly witness domestic violence. Even those who are never directly targeted during domestic violence incidents can still suffer chronically from hyperarousal.[9]

Intuition may be especially useful in situations involving repetitive abuse, such as relational trauma that occurs within an ongoing relationship. Such situations may include emotional, physical, and sexual abuse, as well as abandonment and neglect. Being chronically exposed to one's abuser, or regularly witnessing domestic violence, forces a person to keep strengthening their intuitive skills. In this way, abusive episodes can function as intuitive training sessions. Overall, trauma histories can be shared by family members, so it may be that this factor gives the impression that psi "runs in families."

DISSOCIATION AND TRAUMA

Dissociation is a particular type of trauma response that may also intensify intuition. During trauma, a trigger causes a person to feel emotionally overwhelmed. Once this happens, a person may remove themselves, psychologically, from a situation they cannot stop or physically escape. Through this unconscious survival mechanism, a person may become mentally detached from the scene as well as emotionally numb to their own bodies, thoughts, and memories—and sometimes, even their own identities.

While in a psychologically separated state, a dissociated person can become more focused on their raw, feeling-based, intuitive skills. Intuition gets "kicked on" because it serves an important defensive role during trauma. By using intuition, a person may be able to avoid, prepare for, cope with, and recover from some form of abuse. Through "picking up information" about one's assailant, a person has a better chance of surviving, psychologically and physically. This same concept holds true for children who regularly witness domestic violence and are constantly "reading the room" to get a sense of their own and their loved ones' safety.

* Please note that many highly psychic people do not have traumatic pasts. It's more than possible to develop intuitive abilities without ever having to endure trauma. Likewise, there are also highly psychic people who do not have family members with advanced psi abilities. What I have described are only some known commonalities. People with highly developed psi skills come from many different backgrounds and do not fit into one psychological profile.

Are trance states and dissociation similar?

Professional intuitives often go into a trance state to better access psychic information during their readings. Although both trance states and dissociation are altered states of consciousness, they are qualitatively different in two major ways:

Trance states are *deliberately* induced; dissociation is often *unconscious* and triggered by anxiety.

Trance states are usually *pleasant or neutral;* dissociation can feel *unpleasant or frightening* due to its numbing effects.

Why do people study parapsychology?

People who study the paranormal tend to have a history of personal experiences in this area. Carl Jung, for instance, researched parapsychological topics throughout his career because he personally encountered a large array of paranormal events during his childhood and adulthood. These episodes inspired Jung's lifelong interest in this field; and overall, it was the stockpile of these experiences that prompted him to write in a 1945 letter, "I have seen enough of this phenomenon to convince me entirely of its existence."[10]

The large volume of parapsychological events that Jung experienced ranged from seeing ghosts (both as a child and an adult) to having precognitive dreams, attending seances, experiencing synchronicities, and suffering a near-death episode from a heart attack in 1944.

Jung was introduced to the paranormal at the age of seven when he saw his first ghost. Notably, Jung and his family lived near a cemetery and a dangerous section of the Rhine Falls where many people had drowned.

Thankfully for Jung, he was raised in a family that was open to the paranormal. This is not the case for many people who begin having parapsychological experiences in childhood. Very often, a child grows up in an environment that dismisses or ridicules anything related to this subject, and that child quickly learns to stop speaking about paranormal topics. As those children stay silent, they are left feeling like they must be "crazy" for having these types of experiences. In Jung's case, however, his family was well acquainted with and receptive to the paranormal—so much so that Jung's maternal grandfather believed he was regularly surrounded by ghosts and would spend one day each week speaking with the spirit of his deceased wife.[11] Jung's grandmother was also clairvoyant, and Jung's mother had "strange occurrences" that she wrote about regularly in her journal.[12] Perhaps the largest parapsychological influence on Jung, however, was his cousin who worked as a psychic medium and had Jung regularly attend her sessions. Scholars have speculated that Jung's witnessing his cousin's sessions greatly influenced his psychological theories.

Why is Jung important to study?

The breadth of Jung's work is so profound that it is no exaggeration to say that he was one of the world's most prolific scholars. In addition to his studies in psychiatry and parapsychology, Jung heavily researched spirituality, mythology, symbolism, anthropology, and religion. Overall, Jung greatly expanded upon the ideas of Freud, who was his mentor. Jung developed his own theoretical orientation called Analytical Psychology.

But how, exactly, did these scholars differ in their views of the psyche? Freud's psychology centers around the individual and that person's unconscious, emotional conflicts within their family's dynamics. Jung's psychology, in contrast, envisions both a personal and collective unconscious. Jung theorized that each of us holds archetypes within our psyches. Archetypes are unconscious, universal patterns of thought and images that are shared with all of humanity. One example would be the Shadow Archetype, which represents the darkness within the human psyche. The Shadow contains aspects about ourselves that we often try to ignore. Jung believed that it was our tendency to avoid facing our Shadows that greatly contributed to individual and societal problems.

As with Freudian theory, many Jungian constructs continue to thrive within clinical psychology today. Jungian therapists of all degree levels focus on clients' collective unconscious, archetypes, the Self, the Shadow, the Persona, Anima, Animus, Individuation, synchronicities, and such. And, like his mentor Freud, the impact of Jung's work is so extensive that we can still hear his influence now in our everyday language.

Anyone, for instance, who describes a man as "being in touch with his feminine side" is inadvertently referencing Jung—and, more specifically, Jung's theory that both men and women hold masculine and feminine qualities. The words *introvert* and *extrovert* were coined by Jung and are commonly used today to describe how one manages their social spheres. Job candidates who take the Myers-Briggs Type Indicator are evaluated on a test rooted in Jung's classification of Psychological Types. The Myers-Briggs is used today by 80 percent of Fortune 500 companies and 89 percent of Fortune 100 companies.[13] Even the current lie detector test is based on Jung's word association research.

Jung has had a major impact on many forms of art and culture. Jungian scholar Joseph Campbell brought Jung's concepts to life in new ways, as a major influence on many of today's most popular films, including *Star Wars*, *Batman*, and *Lord of the Rings*. Part of what makes these films so powerful is that they use Jung's construct of the archetypes. The character Darth Vader, for instance, exemplifies The Shadow.

Other performing and visual artists have expressed Jungian ideas through their mediums, as well, such as choreographer Martha Graham and mid-century Abstract Expressionist painter Jackson Pollock, who described himself as a Jungian.[14] Quite simply, Jung is everywhere in our society. For one hundred years and counting, Jung has occupied a rather sizable portion of Western culture's mental space.

A focus on spirituality and psychical research were with Jung throughout every phase of his career. He stands as an extraordinary example of what happens when someone is professionally inspired—even catapulted—by personal experiences. It is hard to imagine the fields of clinical and para-psychology without Jung's colossal footprints.

Why do people mention Freud whenever they talk about Jung?

Many people over the years have told me how much they love Jung but can't stand Freud. But what these people don't realize is that Jung, in all his brilliant, mind-blowing theories, could never have developed his ideas on the unconscious without first being mentored by Freud.

It all started when Jung reached out to Freud about his word association research. On their first meeting, they spoke nonstop for thirteen hours.[15] Their professional relationship lasted five years and was much closer to a father-son dynamic than a "bromance." But their discussions eventually soured. Things went from bad to "worser," and then, radio silence. More to come on the Freud-Jung drama. Stay tuned.

When was parapsychology first studied?

People have been intrigued by parapsychological phenomena since antiquity, but the area first became an object of scientific study in the 1930s. J.B. Rhine, PhD, is considered "the Father of Parapsychology" due to his groundbreaking research at Duke University. Rhine also coined the term extrasensory perception, or ESP.[16]

What are the challenges of parapsychological research?

Many experimental issues arise during parapsychological research that require consideration. For instance, poltergeists, ghosts that purposefully disrupt people's environments by making noises or moving objects, may be impossible to observe and manipulate in the laboratory. Their presence is believed to affect only a specific living and/or working environment, and although parapsychologists can do experimentation on site, they cannot totally exclude confounding variables as they could in a laboratory setting. Researchers who examine poltergeist sightings can only do their best to minimize the intrusion of variables, such as light or temperature changes. Similar experimental problems would arise in other situations, such as a case in which someone sees the spirit of their deceased loved one. Such episodes are very difficult, if not impossible, to replicate under laboratory conditions.

Although problems such as these may plague parapsychological reports, similar experimental issues exist in many clinical psychological studies. Research concerning sexual abuse, for instance, is dependent upon good self-report measures. Thankfully, no laboratory would ever experimentally induce sexual trauma. Researchers who examine the impact of sexual molestation depend entirely upon self-reporting in conjunction with an assessment of how well study participants' symptoms match known patterns of sexual trauma. Thus, while one can say parapsychological research is muddled with experimental problems, I am not convinced that many other clinical psychological studies have any more objective data to rely upon. Was the researcher present during the actual sexual abuse?

Those seeking perfectly controlled, laboratory-based evidence would find themselves equally disappointed by parapsychological and clinical psychological studies. The chemistry laboratory, in which variables are manipulated according to the strictest degree of scientific standards, might better meet these people's expectations.

Are there any gender differences in psychic abilities?

No. It is believed that men and women are equally intuitive. Culturally, however, we tend to associate more intuitive skills with women—which is a mistake, according to Judith Orloff, MD. Orloff is an assistant clinical professor of Psychiatry at University of California, Los Angeles who states that men often lose touch with their intuition because our culture tends to see those feelings as not masculine.[17]

CHAPTER 3

Precognitive Dreams

WITHIN FORTY-EIGHT HOURS OF VISITING SANTA FE, NEW MEXICO, I decided to move there. Six months later, I loaded my little silver car with my belongings and my cat and drove with purpose into the American desert.

Although my private practice and teaching (college students, graduate students, and medical students) were going well in Los Angeles, something felt off. I could not identify the problem, but when I visited the city of Santa Fe, my heart was open to it. I felt captivated by "The City Different" in a way that no other place had affected me. Though I had lived on the East Coast and the West Coast, I was drawn inexplicably to the Southwestern spirit and ruggedly beautiful terrain.

Most of my family and friends were baffled. My father was especially confused, even worried. Over time, I have grown to see how wonderfully unusual my relationship was with him. Conversations flowed naturally from lighthearted to intense, funny to serious, intellectual to absurd. We did not always agree, but our talks were generally easy and consistently filled with love. My father was my favorite person. This was true even in the early years, when I was so terribly angry with him for not believing in me.

Three weeks after my move, my father told me by telephone, "There's something wrong with my blood. The doctors have not figured it out yet. They're still running tests." He was a radiation oncologist who knew all about cancer, so I immediately asked whether he had a blood cancer.

"Nobody knows what the problem is right now," he said.

Later that night, I dreamt of an apocalypse. In my dream, my father died in the worldwide disaster, but my mother, sister, and myself all survived. When I woke that morning, I knew with total certainty that whatever was wrong with my father's blood was going to kill him. As much as I tried, I could not deny this painful awareness. This type of extreme, complete knowledge through intuition was another moment of claircognizance for me.

Throughout the eighteen-month period of his illness (which was, in fact, a blood cancer), I was never able to deny or ignore my certainty that he would die from his disease. I did everything I could to stay positive, but once claircognizance appears, it is impossible to erase the knowledge.

By that time in my life, I had experienced many precognitive dreams. The first time occurred when I was six. We had a two-year-old Golden Retriever I dearly loved, and I dreamt that my dog swallowed a heavy lead ball and died in front of me. I woke up from the dream in the middle of the night, terrified.

The next day, my father and I took the dog for a walk. Suddenly, as if "struck by the gods," she died of a heart attack. As she lay in my arms, my father checked for her heartbeat and pulse. Within minutes, I watched him place her body into the back of the station wagon, to be cremated. My dream of my dog's death the night before her actual passing would be classified as precognitive.

At twenty, I had another precognitive dream in which I was crossing a street late at night when a car traveling at a very high speed nearly killed me. The next night, I was out with a friend in New York City, and as we crossed Third Avenue in the East Village, a car whipped down the street at a high speed, almost running us over.

Precognition can occur unconsciously, such as with these two dreams, or during conscious, waking moments. Either way, precognition involves having knowledge of a future event without ever having had access to information that could have predicted that future occurrence.

It is common for people to confuse the terms precognition and premonition. While they are both variations of psi and are related to one another, a precognition holds very specific knowledge whereas a premonition is a vague, persistent feeling that has the quality of a forewarning. Another distinguishing feature is that a premonition often induces anxiety or dread, and those feelings persist until the actual feared event takes place. Strangely, once the event happens, even if it is tragic, it usually causes feelings of relief. More than likely, relief happens because the mystery is solved, and the mind feels some sense of resolution on that matter.

Researchers who study precognition further explain that a precognition involves cognitive awareness, whereas a premonition contains affective apprehension.[1] Another differentiating factor is the timeframe: precognitive dreams typically happen within a few days of the event, whereas a premonition can last much longer. Premonitions are known to persist for days, weeks, months, or even years.

Precognitions and premonitions, however, serve the same general purpose: they emotionally prepare someone for difficult experiences. Early and present-day researchers have found that precognitions and premonitions tend to center around themes that are highly emotionally intense.[2]

Sometimes, a precognition can function as a specific manifestation of a larger premonition. Imagine, for instance, that I had a general feeling that "something bad" was going to happen to my dog for about a month, and then I dreamt of her death the night before she died. In that one scenario, we see two separate but related psi phenomena around the same situation.

For ten-year-old Eryl Mai Jones, the need for emotional preparation was dire, and perhaps because of this, she had both a premonition and a precognitive dream about the same event. Psychically, Eryl Mai knew tragedy soon would strike her poor coal mining village of Aberfan, Wales.

In the days before the 1966 disaster—a catastrophe in which hard rains would drive a raging, vicious mixture of water, coal silt, and boulders down into the village below—Eryl Mai told her mother, "I'm not afraid to die. I shall be with Peter and June." Mrs. Jones disregarded the possibility that her daughter's statement was a premonition and further discounted the dream Eryl Mai had shared with her the day before: "I went to school and there was no school there. Something black had come down all over it."[3]

One hundred and forty-four people died when the heinous weather concoction obliterated two schoolhouses and eighteen homes that day. The majority of the dead were children.

Tragically, Eryl Mai was one of the 116 children to perish. But who were Peter and June, whom the girl mentioned before the avalanche? They were her classmates, who died with her. The three of them were buried together, among the other children, in a mass grave.

Eryl Mai's case is one of many famous stories of precognitive dreams. Mark Twain, for instance, saw his young, healthy brother's dead body in a casket in a dream shortly before this brother unexpectedly died in an accident. Ten days before his assassination in 1865, Abraham Lincoln had a dream that highly disturbed him. Lincoln told his longtime friend and official biographer, Ward Hill Lamon, the following:

> About ten days ago, I retired very late. I had been up waiting for important dispatches from the front. I soon began to dream. There seemed to be a death-like stillness about me. Then I heard subdued sobs, as if a number of people were weeping. I thought I left my bed and wandered downstairs. There the silence was broken by the same pitiful sobbing, but the mourners were invisible. I went from room to room; no living person was in sight, but the same mournful sounds of distress met me as I passed along. It was light in all the rooms; except every object was familiar to me; but where were all the people who were grieving as if their hearts would break? I was puzzled and alarmed. What could be the meaning of all this? Determined to find the cause of a state of things so mysterious and so shocking, I kept on until I arrived at the East Room, which I entered. There I met with a sickening surprise. Before me was a catafalque, on which rested a corpse wrapped in funeral vestments. Around it were stationed soldiers who were acting as guards; and there was a throng of people, some gazing mournfully upon the corpse, whose face was covered, others weeping pitifully. 'Who is dead in the White House?' I demanded one of the soldiers. 'The President,' was his answer. 'He was killed by an assassin!' Then came a loud burst of grief from the crowd, which awoke me from my dream. I slept no more that night; and although it was only a dream, I have been strangely annoyed by it ever since.

Lamon further wrote,

> This dream was so horrible, so real, and so in keeping with other dreams and threatening presentiments of his, that Mr. Lincoln was profoundly disturbed by it. During its recital he was grave, gloomy, and at times visibly pale, but perfectly calm.[4]

Precognitive or prophetic dreams are actually fairly common. The

National Institutes of Health published a study in 2000 that indicated 17.8 to 38 percent of the population has had at least one precognitive dream.[5] But how exactly do precognitive dreams happen? Let's consider the work of the ultimate giant on dreams: Sigmund Freud.

Back in 1899, thirteen years after Carl Benz invented the car, a time when a well-bred woman would not touch a man without donning a glove, Freud published his masterpiece, *The Interpretation of Dreams*. This book so deeply affected society that it permanently altered how we understand dream life. In his mesmerizing work, Freud mapped out his topographical model of the mind, which delineated different levels of consciousness.[6] Throughout the book, he theorized that each of us has an unconscious force within our psyche that actively prevents us from confronting anxiety-provoking thoughts and feelings. Freud called this unconscious force "repression." According to him, it patrols our psyche twenty-four hours a day, like a watchman on high alert.

Freud initially connected the repression mechanism to sexual trauma, but psychoanalytic theory, over time, has generalized the notion of repression. This emotional filtration process censors out all distressing information from the psyche. Thus, repression serves an essential role in maintaining our mental health. Imagine, for example, trying to focus on work and having painful, intrusive memories suddenly break through into consciousness. Repression prevents this from happening. But it is not perfect: during times of stress, the repression barrier breaks down. Flashbacks seen in post-traumatic stress disorder are clear examples of how disruptive and debilitating breaks in repression can become.

Unfortunately, we pay a steep emotional price for enjoying the benefits of repression. This unconscious mental force may block out emotionally painful memories, but it also holds society's brutal cultural judgments. It is the part of the psyche that causes us to feel shameful and to worry about other people's disapproval. Because of fears of social rejection, repression shapes and restricts how we think and feel. Thoughts like "I must be crazy if I'm hearing spirits" are byproducts of this powerful defense mechanism.

Each night while we sleep, however, we all get a bit of respite from repression's intensity. As we dream, the harsh repression barrier naturally weakens. It is through the softening of this barrier that our psychological defenses lower. Once this occurs, our unconscious and most forbidden wishes emerge in our dreams. More than likely, this lowering of our psychological defenses helps dreamers become more receptive to paranormal information. When the mind is in its more open state, it can no longer fully censor out anxiety-provoking information, whether that involves unpleasant paranormal knowledge, traumatic memories, or something else.

Perhaps repression's most intriguing feature is that it does not go away completely while we sleep. The repression barrier softens, but it does not vanish. Remnants of repression are seen in dream images; for example, in Lincoln's dream, he did not see himself as the corpse. Lincoln's mind, with the help of repression, disguised the corpse's image to allow him to sleep. Similarly, Lincoln did not see the mourners. Had his wife, Mary Todd, been present, it may have startled him enough to wake him, since her image could have suggested to him that he was the corpse. Likewise, another figure noticeably absent from Lincoln's dream was his eleven-year-old son, who died three years before Lincoln's assassination. The presence of his deceased son in the dream would have potentially alarmed Lincoln, because he may have recognized the boy as being a symbol of death. Again, the mind needs a bit of repression to keep the dreamer asleep and sends out disguised dream images to manage the dreamer's anxiety.

In examining the story of Lincoln's dream, and subsequent events, one of the pieces I find most compelling is the emotional intensity of Lincoln's reaction to it the next day. It is possible that Lincoln was so frightened by the dream because, despite his mind's effort to disguise the indicators, he intuitively knew that the dream forecasted his own death. Although the soldier mentioned "the President" in the dream, he never specified which president he was referring to. Lincoln, it seems, intuitively knew the soldier was referring to him.

We can see remnants of the repression barrier in my own apocalyptic dream, as well. It had been a vague, warlike enemy that annihilated most of the planet that killed my father, and not the blood "problem" we discussed earlier that day over the telephone. Repression camouflaged the disease, and converted it into an ambiguous adversary, so I could stay asleep. Had the enemy in my dream been a blood "problem," I may have woken up, mid-dream.

In my opinion, professional psychics deepen their receptivity to paranormal information by loosening their repression barriers while they are in trance states. Edgar Cayce, the most well-known psychic of the twentieth century, was dubbed "The Sleeping Prophet" by the press. During private sessions and group demonstrations, Cayce would lie on a couch, get into a trance state, and provide psychic readings on an array of topics.

Freud, of course, also had a predilection for couches and altered states of consciousness. In fact, Freud initially hypnotized his patients as they laid on his couch, because he believed that while hypnotized, his patients would better access their repressed childhood memories. Soon into this practice, Freud abandoned hypnosis but still had his patients lie on his couch. As they relaxed, Freud invited his patients to free associate and tell him whatever came to mind. Although Freud's psychotherapeutic goals were dramatically different from Cayce's psychic sessions, both men used the same method to weaken the repression barrier.

This same repression barrier can soften during our waking lives, as well. We see it happen during yoga and meditation, and even during rote, unconscious activities such as brushing our teeth, taking a shower or bath, washing dishes, running for extended periods of time, or driving a car on a familiar road. As a result of getting into a less conscious state, we become especially receptive to creative ideas and psychic information. On several occasions, I had to pull my car over to the side of the road and jot down my ideas when sentences for this book suddenly came to my mind. Those car rides unintentionally relaxed the repression mechanism in my mind.

Freud would not be pleased with my linking his theories of repression and the topographical model of the mind with parapsychological phenomena. In fact, if I could travel back in time, and have the good fortune to meet him, my excitement would quickly turn to sadness. Freud would be angry that any psychologist would contaminate his theories with such nonsense. The exploration of spiritual matters displeased Freud so much that he could not fully tolerate Jung, his most prized student, exploring the topic. Indeed, spirituality was one of the major factors that contributed to the severing of all communication between the two trailblazers. That, in addition to Jung's rejection of Freud's dogmatic stance on several subjects, led to the demise of their friendship and Freud's mentoring of Jung.

We see Freud's disgust in this excerpt from his 1909 letter to Jung:

> *Dear Friend, ... It is remarkable that on the same evening that I formally adopted you as an eldest son, anointing you as my successor and crown prince—in partibus infidelium—that then and there you should have divested me of my paternal dignity, and that the divesting seems to have given you as much pleasure as investing your person gave me. Now I am afraid that I must fall back again into the role of father toward you in giving you my views on poltergeist phenomena. I must do this because these things are different from what you would like to think.[7]*

In later sections of the letter, Freud mentions a disputed paranormal experience that occurred while they were together in Freud's famed Berggasse 19 office in Vienna. Freud provides his interpretation of the debated event and ends his letter with:

> *I therefore look forward to hearing more about your investigations of the spook-complex, my interest being the interest one has in a lovely delusion which one does not share oneself. With cordial regards to yourself, your wife and children, Yours, Freud.*[8]

Aside from Freud's inflated ego, and the notion that he was kingly enough to "anoint" anyone to be "prince" of anything, we see Freud's resentment, anger, and disdain jump from the page. And, underneath Freud's rattled ego, we also find his anguish. Freud may have sensed, by this point, that his friendship with Jung would not last. In truth, Freud was not just angry with his "eldest son": he was heartbroken. Just two years after Freud's letter, the two great archeologists of the mind would sever all ties.

Perhaps hardest for Jung was the fact that he had always longed to have intellectual conversations with his own father.[9] In meeting the genius, Freud, Jung had found himself a father figure, someone with whom he could discuss many intellectual matters, someone who might symbolically heal this old wound of his, only to have that possibility disappear.

However short Freud and Jung's time together may have been, it was clearly long enough to permanently change the way our society thinks. It seems neither of them could have intellectually progressed to the same extent without having influenced and pushed back against each other.

As much as Freud would be irritated to hear it, it is probably more accurate to say that he had *mixed* feelings on parapsychology. Initially, Freud was open to the subject, as we see in his highly influential 1901 work, *The Psychopathology of Everyday Life*:

> *...we shall at least have to touch on the question of whether ... there are definitely no such things as true presentiments, prophetic dreams, telepathic experiences, manifestations of supernatural forces and the like...so many detailed observations have been made even by men of outstanding intellect... To my regret I must confess that I am one of those unworthy people in whose presence spirits suspend their*

activity and the supernatural vanishes away, so that I have never been in a position to experience anything myself which might arouse a belief in the miraculous.[10]

Not long thereafter, Freud switched to vehemently criticizing parapsychology, and then to ignoring it altogether. Freud did, however, write a few short essays on parapsychological phenomena (e.g., "The Uncanny," "Dreams and Telepathy," and "A Neurosis of Demonical Possession"), but at this point, it's possible that he was motivated to write these works by the pleasure of potentially discrediting Jung. Regardless of motivation, Freud's focus on parapsychology was quite small, which may reflect how little he valued the topic or how impotent he felt in exploring it.

If my ideas on repression were not enough to upset Freud, then my next thought would make him truly despise me: Parapsychological experiences, in my opinion, defend us, much in the way that repression protects us. Both types of unconscious experiences help maintain our psychological health. Take a moment to consider the major themes in the precognitive dreams I have presented. All those dreams *prepared the dreamer* for some emotionally significant experience. Repression and psychic intuition are both *self-preservative*. Above all, they are *adaptive*.

Like Twain and Lincoln, Jung also famously had precognitive dreams. In describing one of them, Jung wrote:

> *I dreamed that my wife's bed was a deep pit with stone walls. It was a grave, and somehow had a suggestion of classical antiquity about it. Then I heard a deep sigh, as if someone were giving up the ghost. A figure that resembled my wife sat up in the pit and floated upwards. It wore a white gown... I awoke, roused my wife, and checked the time. It was three o'clock in the morning. The dream was so curious that I thought at once that it might signify a death. At seven o'clock came the news that a cousin of my wife had died at three o'clock in the morning.*[11]

The night before his mother's sudden death, Jung also had the following dream.

> *Equally important to me were the dream experiences I had before my mother's death. News of her death came to me while I was staying*

in the Tessin. I was deeply shaken, for it had come with unexpected suddenness. The night before her death I had a frightening dream. I was in a dense, gloomy forest; fantastic, gigantic boulders lay about among huge jungle-like trees. It was a heroic, primeval landscape. Suddenly I heard a piercing whistle that seemed to resound through the whole universe. My knees shook. Then there were crashings in the underbrush, and a gigantic wolfhound with a fearful, gaping maw burst forth. At the sight of it, the blood froze in my veins. It tore past me, and I suddenly knew: the Wild Huntsman had commanded it to carry away a human soul. I awoke in deadly terror, and the next morning I received the news of my mother's passing.[12]

Shortly after his mother passed away, Jung realized he'd had a dream about his father that "presaged" his mother's death. Jung's father had died twenty six years before his mother passed away. In the dream, Jung's father came to see him seeking marital counseling. At the time of the dream, Jung was confused by it. He did not realize the dream was actually forecasting his mother's death. Jung only recognized its precognitive quality *after* his mother died. His parents did not have a happy marriage and in the dream, his father was seeking marital advice because he was going to be reunited with his wife in the afterworld.[13]

Given what I have presented, it may surprise you to learn that not all precognitive dreams predict doom and gloom. Some precognitive dreams occur in the context of positive situations. Another friend of mine relayed a dream in which she saw a friend of hers as pregnant. The woman she had dreamed about had been married for ten years and had never planned on having children. In her dream, my friend saw the wife with a "huge belly." Knowing the pregnancy would be successful, she enthusiastically told the couple that she thought they were going to have a baby. The couple was stunned. They had recently discovered the pregnancy but decided not to tell anyone. The only other person who knew was their doctor. My friend's dream stands in stark contrast to the notion that precognitive dreams only exist to protect the dreamer. Clearly, some precognitive dreams do not serve this defensive role.

LITERAL VS. SYMBOLIC PRECOGNITIVE DREAMS

One theme the reader may have noticed about precognitive dreams is that some are literal, while others are far more symbolic. Over the years, parapsychological researchers have found that, when looked at as a whole, precognitive dreams tend to be literal.[14] Such a finding is consistent with the idea that precognitive dreams primarily function as a form of mental preparation. Thus, by clearly seeing the literal dream content, the dreamer would be in a better position to understand and prepare for some future event. My prophetic dream of crossing the street and nearly being run over by a speeding car is a clear example of this type of directness. Lincoln's and Eryl Mai's dreams are also good, if terribly sad, examples of literal precognitive dreams.

Now, compare the quality of those literal dreams with the far more *symbolic* nature of Jung's precognitive dreams. The dream of my dog's death is another example of such a symbolic precognitive dream. Although she died the following day, it wasn't from swallowing a lead ball, as I'd witnessed in my dream. Instead, the dog jumped up to greet our neighbor, collapsed, and died instantly at my feet.

Regardless of whether precognitive dreams are literal or symbolic, when analyzing dream images, it is essential to consider the context of the dreamer's life and the basic nature of the dreamer. Much of Jung's writing and clinical work focused on the analysis of symbolism, so it is especially likely that any of Jung's dreams, precognitive or otherwise, would be richly layered with symbolism. As a psychiatrist, theorist, and scholar, Jung swam in metaphor daily.

In my dream, it is logical that my dog would have died in the context of play; as a six-year-old, play activities would naturally have been at the forefront of my mind. Another aspect to consider about the symbolism of my dream is that, more than likely, my parents warned me against allowing the dog to have dangerous objects: she could swallow them. Their warnings may have prompted my mind to conjure up the lead ball image. Why my unconscious specifically turned the ball into lead is unclear, but it may be related to my having recently seen the movie *Superman*. Lead is problematic for the main character, Superman: he cannot see through it. In my dream, lead is so bad and so powerful that it kills my dog.

Notably, when she was necropsied prior to cremation, the veterinarian found she had suffered from an enlarged heart due to a congenital defect. Thus, my six-year-old unconscious had centered in on the notion that there was some heaviness inside my dog—an abnormal weight that would kill her. Although not a lead ball, her enlarged heart was an oval-shaped object that, in fact, weighed more than it should. Unfortunately, because young children between the ages of two and seven years old are prone to magical thinking, I believed that I murdered our family dog. In my six-year-old psyche, if I dreamt about something the night before it happened, I must have caused it. Of course, as I grew older, I came to understand that the dog's death was not my doing.

PRECOGNITIVE DREAMS IN CHILDREN

Although stories of children with precognitive dreams are common, I have had great difficulty finding peer-reviewed precognition studies in child populations. It is unclear precisely why there is such a lack of research in this subgroup. It is possible that the children's various stages of cognitive development, difficulties with dream recall, and short attention spans are deemed too problematic for precognition researchers.

My sense as to why children may be more prone to precognitive dreams is that children are less emotionally defended as compared to adults; therefore, they are better able to access paranormal information in general. More specifically, a child's repression barrier is naturally immature, helping them feel less aware of societal pressures. Young children, in particular, have even less awareness of cultural norms and expectations. This is why a three-year-old would show less repression in their dreams than would a nine-year-old.

THE EVOLUTIONARY ROLE OF PRE-COGNITIVE DREAMS

Professor Emeritus at Cornell University, Daryl Bem, PhD, calls precognition "magical" because of how it violates our understanding of the physical world.[15] In his highly successful article published by the *Journal of Personality and Social Psychology* in 2011, "Feeling the Future: Experimental Evidence for Anomalous Retroactive Influences on Cognition and Affect," Bem reported the results of nine experiments he conducted on precognition with over one thousand participants. In eight of nine experiments, Bem successfully showed evidence of precognition. But how did Bem examine precognition, which we know confounds researchers?

In one of his nine studies, Bem recruited one hundred Cornell University undergraduates through the Psychology Department (fifty females; fifty males). On a screen, all the participants were shown images of two curtains, side by side. Participants were instructed to click on the curtain that they thought had a picture behind it. (One of the curtains had a blank wall behind it, while the other curtain had a photo.) When the participants opened the curtains, they immediately saw whether they had chosen correctly. In several instances, the pictures the participants found behind the curtain were of couples engaged in consensual sexual acts.

Bem's main psi hypothesis was that his study's participants would be able to identify the location of the hidden erotic picture significantly better than chance.[16] Bem sought to examine precognition this way because presentiment studies have shown that people can anticipate erotic or negative stimuli before they occur.[17] Overall, Bem sees this type of anticipation as evolutionarily advantageous for reproduction and survival of the species.[18]

Not only did Bem find evidence of precognition in eight of his nine studies, but he also further explained that the odds the data are the result of random chance or statistical flukes are about seventy-four billion to one.[19]

FOUNDING PARENTS OF THE FIELD

Long before Professor Bem, Joseph Banks (J.B.) Rhine, PhD, conducted seminal paranormal studies at Duke University from 1930 to 1965. His main areas of focus included precognition, clairvoyance, telepathy, and psychokinesis (moving objects solely with the power of the mind). Famously, many of Rhine's participants were tested with a deck of twenty-five Zener cards that each contained one of five symbols. (The cards were created by Karl Zener, PhD, Rhine's colleague at the university.) During these studies, the subject would face the experimenter behind an opaque barrier and choose a card from a shuffled pack of twenty-five cards. The experimenter would note the symbol on the card and record the participant's guess of that symbol.

Rhine also worked alongside his wife and colleague, Louisa Rhine, PhD, who performed her own parapsychological investigations. Like her husband, (and, separately, Jung), Dr. Louisa Rhine discovered that the vast majority of parapsychological cases concerned major events such as deaths, personal crises, illnesses, accidents, births, and marriages.[20] In one of her publications, Dr. Louisa Rhine referenced a case in which an elderly woman dreamt that her daughter was pregnant, which was later confirmed.[21]

Dr. Louisa Rhine also showed that although precognition can happen during wakefulness, it is far more likely to occur during dreams. Her studies, and other investigations since then, indicate that seventy-five percent of precognition episodes occur while someone is asleep.[22] When explaining why precognition primarily occurs in dreams, Dr. Louisa Rhine noted how the idea of obtaining information about a future event might feel so bizarre, and so disturbing to people, that the information may only enter someone's mind while their intellectual defenses are down.[23]

Jung learned of the Rhines' work at Duke University and was rather impressed with their findings. He became an enthusiastic supporter of their work. Jung believed the researchers were proving that at least a part of the psyche was not subject to the laws of space, time, and causality.[24]

As with Freud, Jung communicated with J.B. Rhine primarily through letters. For those curious readers who want to see large portions of the Jung-Rhine correspondence, I recommend reading the work, *C.G. Jung Letters, Volume 1, 1906–1950.*

It is noteworthy for our purposes that, in one letter, Jung described to Rhine two separate paranormal instances he personally encountered and which took place within days of each other. One concerned a knife that "exploded" and broke apart in four places while inside a cabinet. The second concerned a ninety-year-old thick wooden table that spontaneously split open with a thunderous boom.

Rhine responded to Jung's letter by asking him for a photograph of the broken knife. He also shared some of the data he had discovered in his laboratory on telepathy, clairvoyance, and trance states, and he communicated his respect for Jung by stating that he had "a great deal to learn from [him]."[25]

In another correspondence, Rhine asked Jung if Duke University could receive the actual knife Jung had written about. Jung did not send Rhine the knife, but he did send him a photograph of it which remains in Duke University's collection today. In general, Jung was hesitant to show this knife to the public out of concern for being seen as "crazy."[26]

What a relief it must have been for Jung to have found Rhine. In Rhine, Jung discovered his first parapsychological colleague and peer. Rhine's fascination and curiosity with Jung's paranormal experiences stood in stark contrast to the types of reactions Jung had received throughout his life so far regarding this topic—whether from Freud, his other colleagues, or friends. As Jung described, "I came up against the steel of people's prejudice and their utter incapacity to admit unconventional possibilities. I found this even with my closest friends. To them, all this was far worse than my preoccupation with theology."[27]

For Rhine, having the positive feedback and encouragement from the world-renowned Jung must have been greatly validating. I imagine that

Rhine may have faced the same ridicule and isolation Jung endured. In the 1930s, these men were a source of much needed support for each other.

Although Rhine is considered controversial today, he was highly regarded by Duke University at the time, which saw enough scientific merit in his work to fund his laboratory continuously for thirty-five years. There is an exhibit today on Rhine in Duke University's library system. Throughout his time at the college, Rhine collected an astonishing amount of data. It is believed that he conducted 90,000 parapsychological experiments while on staff.[28]

After his work at the university, Rhine founded the Rhine Research Center in Durham, North Carolina, which is still in operation. He also founded the Parapsychological Association and the peer-reviewed *Journal of Parapsychology*, which publishes on psi phenomena such as precognition, clairvoyance, telepathy, psychokinesis, as well as other topics. Both professional resources remain active today.

Rhine was highly receptive to Jung's experiences. One gets the sense that Jung had only seen this same degree of openness about the paranormal within his family. And I wonder if Rhine's nonjudgmental stance metaphorically felt like home for Jung. As I think about that possibility some more, I am remembering the fact that Jung's childhood home was next to the Rhine River. Something seems more than coincidental about that. It seems rather beautiful.

CHAPTER 4

Owl Medicine

WITH STUNNING BEAUTY, SHE SPRANG FROM MY GLOVED HAND, SLICED into my scalp, and ripped a gash in my leather jacket. Shocked by the Great Horned Owl, I stood in disbelief.

Remember, the handler always stays in charge.

Never one to miss a good wisecrack, my boss Tom laughed beside me. "Welcome to the club."

That jab was the bird's signature move, Tom told me. She had nailed every handler she'd ever worked with. I was now on her list of humans.

The wounds she gave me that day were minor, but they were also clear signs of how formidable the Great Horned Owl can be. It took only seconds for that animal to attack and draw blood. So effective is this hunter that when her talons are clenched, they require a force of twenty-eight pounds to open.[1]

As a human, I was not her typical victim. Those damned souls are other birds of prey, rodents, scorpions, frogs, and even small cats and dogs.

My dicey day with that beautiful beast took place several years after I began volunteering at a wildlife center near Santa Fe. When I first visited the center, I decided I wanted to work as a handler. I had volunteered for wildlife organizations before, though only as a fundraiser, and I felt it was time to get my hands dirty. Little did I know how dirty they would become.

The center welcomed me as a volunteer. I was allowed to clean cages—and nothing else. For eight long months, every Friday, for four hours, I cleaned the shit of hawks, owls, eagles, falcons, kestrels, goshawks, magpies, turkey vultures, ospreys, ravens, and foxes. Together, with a group of other cleaners, we shit-cleaned regardless of the weather: rain, sleet, snow, excessive heat.

Each mew, where the birds were housed individually, was sizeable, and every square inch needed tending. Eagles liked to spray their shit high up on the walls. The osprey was so testy that we often cleaned her cage in pairs. I once saw a cleaner bolt from a kestrel's cage, blood streaming down her face. The bird inside had "footed" her with its talons.

On bitterly cold winter days, our hands were frozen solid; mats covered in shit needed to be scraped and hosed, and water always seeped into our gloves. Everything about that job was difficult, but I had never been that close to wild birds before, and the teachings were tremendous.

What makes a girl from the suburbs of New York City clean cages for free in the desert? Since childhood, I have been fascinated by wild animals. To me, they are spiritual beings. I see them as intermediaries between the physical plane and the spiritual world.

I was grateful to be so close to those animals, if only as their cleaner. Instead of marveling at a hawk as she flew above my head in an open field, I could be with her inside her enclosure. I was with Spirit in a way that I had never previously known.

As a cleaner, I became acutely aware of how my energy affected the birds—positively or negatively. I became emotionally present to a heightened degree, which strengthened my intuition. The birds' safety and my own safety depended on my ability to read their needs quickly and accurately. On one level, it was not dissimilar to what I did at work: as a psychologist, I was constantly sensing my clients' emotional cues. However, their basic safety was never at risk. Nor was mine. Inside a cage with a wild animal, safety was conditional. There was no room for error.

A core value was instilled by the organization that magnified those lessons: *"The bird is always right."* If a non-releasable bird got out of an enclosure, it was the volunteer's fault. If a bird fell to the ground, it was the volunteer's fault. Anything that went wrong in the presence of the volunteer was the volunteer's fault. This made sense to me. After all, no one was going to put the birds on trial.

Our facility was a rescue, rehabilitation, and release center that treated injured, sick, and orphaned wild animals. Most of the animals who came to us stayed only briefly before being successfully released back into the New Mexican ecosystem. A small portion were euthanized. But some of the animals treated by the center were stuck somewhere in the middle. They could be partly rehabilitated: these birds *could* fly, but not well enough. They *could* walk, but not fast enough to escape a predator. And some of these "in between" animals had a disposition which suggested that they potentially could be handled. These animals were kept as "educational ambassadors" by the center. It was their cages that I tended.

After eight months, all the cleaners—including me—were invited to start training in the Handler/Educator program. They told each of us to pick a "starter bird." On the starter list were certain falcons, hawks, owls, turkey vultures, and kestrels—birds known to be easier to handle. Without hesitating, I chose an owl.

Believe it or not, I did *not* know that I had chosen one of the largest symbols in nature of the paranormal. I had never read *Harry Potter;* nor had I studied much of anything about owls. (My work with the owl began over a decade ago, when owl imagery/merchandise was less common than it is today.) However, almost immediately, I began having particular, perhaps unusual feelings whenever I was around the owls. When I was done cleaning their enclosures, I didn't want to leave them. I missed them when I went home. Even more bizarre, I wanted to curl up and sleep inside their cages with them. I wanted to stay with them through the night. Take care of them if they needed me. Was I feeling like their mother? Their sister? Their servant? Their pet? What the fuck?!

My attachment to my owl—and to the other owls I cared for and cleaned up after—continued to grow, which was helpful, because the rules and duties for the Handler/Educator program were extensive and required considerable perseverance. To become certified to handle the owl, I had to show that I could perform all the requirements. This entailed two portions: First, during an evaluation, I would need to physically demonstrate with the bird all the necessary steps for handling. Second, I would need to pass an oral exam whereby I would be tested on the animal's basic scientific information.

And so, I began to prepare for my introduction to bird handling. I was tremendously excited and chose Racho, a Barred Owl. But several weeks into our getting to know each other, BAM! Tragedy struck. Something terrible happened. The bird, who had sustained a head injury in the past, suffered a seizure while training with a different handler. He survived the incident, but Tom permanently removed all his handlers and assigned me a different owl.

On my first day of working with my new bird, I broke a basic rule: *"Whatever you do, don't fall in love with the bird."*

Yeah. That rule. That's the one I broke.

Perhaps it was the way Roja looked at me with her gigantic, saucer eyes. She was an Eastern Screech Owl with streaky orange, yellow, white, and brown feathers that laid straight against her tiny, 6-ounce frame.

Roja had come to the center injured after colliding with a car. But before that, this exquisite, tiny owl with golden soulful eyes was a proud resident of the forest. In the days of her freedom, she would perch herself on a tree branch, high above the ground, and rotate her neck up to 270 degrees to see her surroundings. Although her eyes were stunning, Nature forgot to make them perfect. Magnificent but fixed in their sockets, Roja's eyes never gave her good peripheral sight.

In the days and nights before her crash, Roja relied mostly upon her hearing. Like any owl, she was one of the world's greatest listeners. She hunted primarily by sound because, in a beautiful display of Darwinian adaptation, nearly every part of Roja's little body was built for listening. Her satellite dish-shaped face and asymmetrical ears would triangulate sound. The wondrous noises of her favorite scampering, scuttling prey were funneled directly into her brain. Even the stiff feathers of the ruff encircling Roja's face were designed by Nature to magnify and channel sounds toward her. Roja worked hard every day in the wild to keep herself fed. She would hear live prey scurrying beneath the soil and grab the animal by surprise through the dirt. Sometimes, she would grasp her prey as it ran along the ground. Other times, she'd catch it as it soared through the air. Roja would go hungry if she did not work. Driven, focused, guided by sound, Roja's acuity was so strong that she could hear a mouse stepping on a twig fifty feet away. Small but fierce, Roja was a silent hunter. Her comb-like, serrated feathers broke up the air as she flew,[2] and this was how she shocked her prey. Most victims never saw this predator charge. So silent was Roja that even she couldn't hear her own wing flaps. Nature's gift of serrated feathers removed all distracting sounds.

When Roja captured her food, she often ate the animal's body whole, headfirst. While there might be days when she would shred apart her prey's body and eat just its head, on most days, the prey entered Roja in one piece.

Six hours after eating, Roja would cough up her prey's indigestible body parts—fur, teeth, bones, and claws—as pellets. Intuitively, Roja understood what was toxic.

Later, during her captivity, Roja would not eat in front of me, even when I fed her. Some part of her knew she would be defenseless.

Long after I had completed my Handler Training, there was a day when she coughed up a pellet in front of a group of children. Disgusted and thrilled, they shrieked with horror and delight. What a performance Roja gave that day.

The children would not forget her. They would grow older and want to protect wild animals because an Eastern Screech Owl had come to their classroom, and they had gotten to meet her. Roja would remain in their memories because she was not simply a picture in a book, nor a distant creature perched atop a tree. That afternoon, Roja, all six ounces of her, stood on a glove in front of the chalkboard where their teacher wrote math problems and grammar rules. She was steps from where the girls and boys passed notes back and forth and giggled before recess. Roja was in the very room where they were learning of the Red Coats invading Virginia and the number of American lives lost in battle.

Roja, fluff and hoot, was in their "house."

But I am getting ahead of the story: It was not always so easy with Roja. It was hard work. In the beginning, it was new, scary, and wonderful at once.

THE PREAMBLE

During the first stage with Roja, I focused solely on helping her feel more comfortable with me. To get her used to my presence and my voice, I sat inside her enclosure and read aloud to her. No *Wuthering Heights*. No *Gone with the Wind*. No *Fifty Shades of Grey*. Just the trusty Handler Manual. I needed the intel, and my poor "captive" got stuck hearing details about keys and cage latches.

In the next phase, I crouched down with my bare hands open. For an owl in Roja's predicament—an educational bird regularly touched by staff wearing gloves—the most frightening thing I could bring inside her enclosure was a handler's glove. Once Roja saw my glove, she would know that our real *pas de deux* was about to start. My glove was like a bell for Pavlov's dog. So, I delayed the glove for some time.

Little by little, Roja came to see that I was not there to harm her. As we trained, I constantly watched her signals. When Roja showed signs of distress, such as panting, I stopped and left immediately. The work could resume another day. Steadily, carefully, we went along, each of us reading and intuiting the other.

Patience is one of the greatest lessons these sacred, winged creatures taught me. Like any driven person, I wanted my goals to happen within a reasonable timeline. And I was anxious to begin working hands-on with my owl. But bird training has its own time. To me, it is spiritually paced.

As I progressed with Roja, I also learned how to be what I call "lovingly in charge." Often, handlers get into trouble with wild animals by being either too passive, which may cause the animal to become aggressive, or too domineering, which can result in the animal fighting back. I'd put my money on the animal in that scuffle!

Eventually, it was time to wear my first layer of defense against the raptor's talons: my glove. But even then, I was on high alert as Roja shared her signals with me. Although I oversaw her safety, only she knew when she was willing to sit on my glove. Remaining patient with a wild animal is like actively listening to a client during therapy. By staying with the client in their associations and feelings, I am giving them the support and freedom to pace themselves. A client intuitively and unconsciously knows when they are ready for growth, just as a well-trained "starter bird" knows how to get on the glove but will sit on that new person's fist only when they are ready.

And that day came for Roja.

THE APPROACH

Advancing toward a captive, wild bird, especially while wearing a glove, is not easy. I needed to read Roja's signals even better than before. Wild birds are naturally resistant to being handled, and each day, I had to figure out just how oppositional she felt. Was she reasonably annoyed but okay with my approaching her? Or was she so agitated that a disaster might happen if I pursued? Making it even trickier, sometimes the bird would position herself high up in her cage, and I would need a ladder to coax her down.

But, as I spent more time with Roja, I grew able to get her to step onto my glove. Regardless of where she positioned herself inside the mew, it all became easier.

THE JESS

After I could repeatedly get Roja onto my glove, I then needed to jess her. Every educational bird already was fitted with loose metal rings around their ankles. I needed to thread leather ties called jesses through those metal parts on Roja and attach the jesses to a swivel and leash. Once this equipment was set, the bird would not be able to escape my glove.

THE BATE

Even though a bird wearing attached jesses cannot escape a handler's glove, the bird nevertheless often tries. It will try to escape. As a winged being, its inclination is to want to fly. The action of a jessed bird trying to fly is called a bate. When a bird on a glove has been spooked by a sound, it will bate and bate hard. As they bate, they beat their wings and jolt and swoop their bodies forward and downward. It is their desperate leap for freedom. A moment of instinct, a bird's bate is its natural, if powerful, attempt to reenter nature. It is the time when they beg most to be themselves.

To protect their bird, the handler must safely control the bate and calmly get the bird back on the glove. "Make your arm as stiff as a branch," Tom told me.

These were wise words, and yet I hated the bate. Never once did I get used to it. Roja could hurt herself, which would devastate me. She could hang herself upside down; she could exhaust herself. A frenzied bate could put her into a state of uncontrolled fury, which might be dangerous to her. Every time she bated, my heart seemed to stop. Yes, I could gently bring her back on my glove, but at no point could I take away her terror. All I could do was try to prevent anything that might set off a bate and help calm Roja.

THE RETURN

After each handling session, as much as I longed to bring Roja home with me, she needed to go back to her cage. All the steps had to be reversed—removing her jesses and leash, detaching her safely from my glove, removing myself carefully from her enclosure.

After I could repeatedly, and reliably, complete these steps—which took months—I was given my tests. Finishing everything got me certified to present at schools and libraries and other events. But a handler could only be certified per animal. If I wanted to handle others, I would need to start all over again.

Which is exactly what I did.

HUECO AND SANTIAGO

After several months of training on Roja, I added a Burrowing Owl named Hueco to my handling duties. As with Roja, Hueco also had an unrecoverable wing injury. After a couple of years of working with the two of them, I added Santiago, the Great Horned Owl. Bird after bird, I wanted more owls.

Santiago was the beautiful monster who took a piece of my scalp and drew my blood. Originally believed to be male, Santiago shocked the staff seven years into her stay by laying an egg. She came to the center as a hatchling because she and her nest mates were shot with a BB gun while their mother was hunting. Santiago was the only owlet to survive, and her mother abandoned the nest.

At the center, Santiago developed quite the reputation. Specifically, she liked to attack her handlers' eyes, and since I was committed to keeping mine attached to my face, I wore special glasses for protection.

Although grumpy and prone to violence, Santiago made an excellent foster mother. Whenever the center received injured and orphaned Great Horned owlets, they boarded up Santiago's mew and she, in private, taught the baby birds all they needed to know to survive in the wild. Over the course of more than thirty years, Santiago personally saved hundreds of owlets from starvation and predation.

What is extraordinary to me is that, without prior knowledge, I was repeatedly drawn to perhaps the world's most parapsychological creature. Strangely, it took a while for me to discover this.

As Handler/Educators, we were given strict instructions on what to say to the public. Only the animals' scientific and environmental roles were to be discussed. Similarly, audience members' comments that veered into non-scientific directions were to be politely redirected. As a good Handler, I followed these rules. For a long time into my handling work, and partly because of my rule-following, I did not study the owl's mythology and symbolism. While I already knew owls were symbols of the moon and the night (most owls hunt at night because they are nocturnal—hence the phrase "night owl" and their association with the night), there was so much more to discover.

To my amazement, I found a saddening history of owls throughout literature. Many cultures, across millennia, have feared and even hated the owl. After reviewing the facts, one gets the sense that this extraordinary creature, with over 200 different species around the globe,[3] has been feared on every continent (except Antarctica, of course, where they do not live).

Why? What is it about these birds that evokes such terror and anger? As I dug deeper into the material, I found the answers could be organized into three categories: the animals' associations with death; female empowerment; and witches.

DEATH
(MY MOST UPLIFTING SUBTITLE YET)

Starting more than five thousand years ago in Ancient Egypt, owls, also known by the Egyptians as "birds of death," were seen as symbols of mourning, evil, and sickness.[4] Yet, despite the fear with which Egyptians viewed owls, Egyptologists have also discovered countless mummified owls inside the Pharaohs' tombs. Indeed, the ancient Egyptians held a mixture of disparate beliefs about these birds. At some times, they saw them as evil; while in other periods, though, they viewed these birds as protectors against wickedness. Owl mummies were used to ward off evil spirits,[5] and archeologists have found many amulets or talismans shaped as owls inside tombs from the fifth century AD. They were placed there to protect the wearers from dangers in the afterlife.[6] The Barn Owl species was a particularly common hieroglyph,[7,8] often found carved into Egyptian writing tablets. At the Metropolitan Museum of Art in New York, there is a spectacular relief of an owl carved onto a plaque which dates from 400–30 BC.[9]

In 332 BC, Alexander the Great conquered Egypt,[10] marking the beginning of the Ptolemaic Period. As a result of the Greeks' new presence in Egypt, we also find Greek images within ancient Egyptian artwork of this time. The Greek god of silence and secrecy, Harpokrates,[11] for instance, was often depicted in ancient Egypt with an owl—his sacred bird and lunar deity.[12]

Yet, regardless of who ruled ancient Egypt, owls were consistently associated with death. Although this finding is quite negative today, during ancient Egyptian times, death was a subject of extreme fascination—so much so that it took on the quality of a fixation. Consider the amount of time and the number of people it took to create just one of the Pharaoh's tombs. Think of all the mummies, sarcophagi, wall paintings, carvings, funerary statues, and such made to go inside *just one tomb*. Now, multiply all that hard work across *all* the Pharaohs' and nobility's tombs.

Used as instruments for the Pharaohs' eternity, the owls' cohabitation with the ancient Egyptians must have been downright grueling. Indeed, by the Ptolemaic period, thousands of owls were relentlessly hunted, suffocated, beheaded, and then mummified and deified.[13] Chased down and sacrificed for the Pharaohs' journey into the next world, the owls who lived back then must have had a difficult life.

And, as I learned of the viciousness in which these birds were hunted, I found myself reading over and over one basic fact: the owls were not simply killed and left in tombs; they were properly mummified. Their bodies were methodically dissected, salted for many days, carefully wrapped in linen, and buried inside special containers. This was done because the ancient Egyptians did not simply fear these winged creatures; they went through the trouble of tending to their bodies and taking great ritualistic care because, underneath it all, they saw the animal as sacred.

Unsurprisingly, owls appeared in the ancient Egyptians' Book of the Dead, which was not a book in today's sense, but rather a series of ancient funerary spells or prayers that were created to help the deceased travel through the afterlife and unite with Osiris, the god of death and rebirth.[14] The Getty Museum in Los Angeles has in its collection seven papyri scrolls and twelve linen mummy wrappings from this "book." Countless authors contributed to the Book of the Dead over a period lasting more than a thousand years. This guidebook for navigating a better and safer journey through the afterworld underscores the constant, obsessional focus the ancient Egyptians held on the afterlife.

Since ancient Egypt, many other cultures have also seen owls as harbingers of death or symbols of death. Several Native American tribes, such as the Lakota, Omaha, Cheyenne, Fox, Ojibwa, Menominee, Cherokee, Cree, and Pueblo consider owls to be embodied spirits of the dead, symbols of evil, and representations of the Skeleton Man, the god of death.[15,16] But, if this god of death is a masculine figure for certain Native American tribes, then the next symbol for the owl is a distinctly feminine one.

FEMALE EMPOWERMENT

Even more frightening than death for some people is the idea of a powerful woman, which brings us to the second category or reason why the bird has been feared and hated across time. The owl's connection with empowered females most likely began with Athena, the ancient Greek goddess of war and wisdom.

But the ancient Greeks did not hate Athena. They lauded her so greatly that they named their booming metropolis—the birthplace of democracy, philosophy, mathematics, astronomy, medicine, ethics, alchemy, theater, chemistry, and humanities—after her. They called their extraordinary creation Athens. The contempt for strong women would come later, with a different ancient, mythic female.

Countless scholars throughout history tell us the owl was Athena's sacred bird. Ancient Greek artworks consistently show the goddess with her owl, which is almost always a small species. The little owl's connection with Athena is so well-established that the bird appears in scenes of Athena's birth and even replaces the goddess herself at times.[17] Notably, Hueco, the Burrowing Owl I handled, got its scientific name from the goddess and is technically referred to as an *Athene Cunicularia*. Hueco is a descendant of Athena's owl.

Zoologist, ethologist, and sociobiologist Desmond Morris, PhD, tells us that ancient Greek generals used owls to inspire their troops. It was believed that if Athena appeared to the soldiers in the shape of an owl, Greek forces would triumph in war. This idea was taken so seriously that one Greek general kept an owl in a cage and released it over his troops to give them courage.[18]

More than a symbol of wartime triumph, the owl was also seen as wise and clairvoyant by the ancient Greeks who chose the bird as the guardian of the Acropolis. Today, Kennesaw State University mirrors the ancient Greeks' perspective in their rationale for choosing the owl as their mascot: Perched on Athena's shoulder, the owl revealed truths and omens to her and symbolized the second sight.[19]

Beyond being regarded as symbols of victory, wisdom, and clairvoyance, Athena and her little owl also appeared on ancient Greek currency as symbols of fortune and fertility.[20,21] Morris instructs that for hundreds of years, from the sixth to the first centuries BC, Athenian coins were minted with the image of the goddess on one side and the owl on the other.[22] Six thousand such coins were recovered along the archeological site of Tell el-Maskhuta in the eastern part of the Nile Delta.[23]

Refusing to be upstaged by the Greeks, the ancient Romans had an equivalent to Athena whom they called Minerva. Although Minerva was a wise and warring goddess, also with a little owl beside her, the ancient Romans' drive to compete against the Greeks was so strong that they gave Minerva additional attributes. Thus, Minerva also became the goddess of weaving, medicine, crafts, and commerce. Yet, she continued to be depicted with an owl. Artworks throughout history, such as Rembrandt van Rijn's painting *Minerva* circa 1655 show the Roman goddess with her owl.[24]

WITCHES

The owl's association with forceful women did not end with Athena and Minerva. It was from the next iconic female, a woman with a decidedly dark and more ominous flavor, that the idea of a courageous and powerful woman turned scary—things went from plain evil to seriously, really, absolutely, flat-out ridiculously, wickedly evil.

She was a "witch," a "night monster," a "she-devil," a "night hag," and she had a name that would translate as "Screech Owl."[25,26] The ancients called her Lilith, and she haunted the Biblical Hebrews and early Christian Gnostics like no one else.

Far ahead of her time, and deeply pissed, Lilith was one tough lady. As the legendary first wife of Adam, she refused to be submissive to him, seeing herself as his equal. Demanding her independence, Lilith, perhaps the world's first feminist refugee, fled the Garden of Eden as "The Original Bitch Goddess."[27]

Raphael Patai, PhD, Cultural Anthropologist and Visiting Professor at University of Pennsylvania, Columbia University, New York University, and Princeton University, specialized in Jewish history and wrote hundreds of scholarly articles and dozens of books throughout his long, celebrated academic career. Patai wrote extensively on Lilith, chronicling her as:

> *The paramour of lascivious spirits...the bride of Samael the demon King... a fully developed evil she-demon. ... [She was] believed to have been a harlot and a vampire who, once she chose a lover, would never let him go, without ever giving him real satisfaction. [She] had no milk in her breasts. ...* **She was beautiful, and nude with wings and owl-feet. She stands erect on two reclining lions which are turned away from each other and are flanked by owls.** *On her head she wears a cap embellished by several pairs of horns. ... This is no longer a lowly she-demon, but a goddess who tames wild beasts* **and as shown by the owls on the reliefs, rules by the night.**[28]

And if Patai's description of this legendary witch doesn't sound malicious enough, other scholars tell us that Lilith would not only seduce men, but she would also bear them a demon offspring and then, as "the incarnation of all that is opposed to life and motherhood,"[29] kill the infant. Sexy but evil, powerful enough to leave a man and live on her own—all while being psychically talented? It's no wonder the ancient people feared this winged goddess.

Although Lilith is only partly responsible for the owl's negative associations with the paranormal, it is from her story that we see a significant increase in people's fear of owls. (We also see some of the roots of why people would burn and execute witches throughout history.) Once hailed by the ancient Greeks for its clairvoyance, once revered as the guardian of the Acropolis, this same bird, with the same set of psychic associations, at the same time, was sinister in the ancient people's minds.

"So unfair!" I huffed to myself as I read. "It's not like these animals invented death!"

Steadily, owing to their associations with death and a seemingly demonic "bitch" woman, owls also came to be seen as malevolent reincarnations of the dead,[30] manifestations of the devil, and messengers of witches and sorcerers,[31,32] whether spells are performed with negative intentions or not. Curiously, many cultures have also nicknamed owls "cats with wings,"[33] something so intriguing when we consider that both animals are the favorite pets of witches. Both creatures are believed to be symbols of the night, mystery, and femininity.

Spiritual writers tell us that owls help psychics by serving as guides through the Akashic Records, which are believed to be a collection of the world's spiritual history. The intuitives Edgar Cayce and Nostradamus are thought to have accessed the Akashic Records for their readings.[34]

Beyond these three major categories—owls as symbols of death, female empowerment, and witches—I found additional fascinating and overarching themes in the symbology of owls.

WISDOM

The idea that owls are symbols of wisdom and keepers of ancient knowledge is likely connected with the bird's unusual eating habits. The fact that the prey enters the owl headfirst has been seen, symbolically, as the owl's taking in the prey's energy, wisdom, and teachings.[35] Further linked to wisdom is the notion that the animal coughs up as pellets whatever it senses is destructive or unnecessary. Spiritual writers see the owl's regurgitation as a metaphor and model for human emotional processing, whereby the bird takes in and retains important lessons and expels whatever is not helpful.[36]

The bird's extraordinary night vision is also connected to its being seen as wise, because the animal can see what is typically hidden or purposely concealed in darkness. Owls are, therefore, considered seers of truths.

Additionally, the animal's ability to fly silently is further linked to wisdom. Writers throughout history have long taught on the advantages of staying silent. Silence has been associated with thoughtfulness, self-awareness, intuition, patience, and emotional stability. As such, silence has been an essential part of various spiritual practices for thousands of years.

INTUITION

Most owls are nocturnal, and their ability to hunt in the dark, primarily by sound, is likely the main reason why the owl has been seen as a symbol of intuition.

As an exceptional listener, the owl models the importance of listening to things beneath the surface. It also shows the importance of hearing those around us and reminds us to listen deeply to ourselves. Listening with great intensity often means hearing information we would rather ignore. But the owl models the value of hearing everything, including unpleasant news.

EXTRACTORS OF SECRETS

In ancient Rome, owls were called "extractors of secrets."[37] Back then, it was believed that if you left an owl's body part or feather on a sleeping person, they would reveal their private thoughts.[38]

As I learned more about the owl's place in mythology and culture, it became clearer to me why so many people have feared these birds across millennia. Symbols of death, female empowerment, war, wisdom, intuition, witchcraft, and sorcery, owls could not be easy creatures for societies to embrace. Within their intense and mysterious nature, owls reflect life's more difficult aspects.

Those who fear the owl often describe their vocalizations as "spooky." And yet, for those of us who find these birds captivating and magical, their noises are some of the world's most extraordinary sounds. Only a couple of months ago, while vising Northern California, I listened to a Great Horned

Owl hoot from a tree for thirty minutes at midnight. The bird's calls were so beautiful that I nearly cried. I was left spellbound.

My work with the owls stirred a dormant part of my psyche. Soon into my time with these winged creatures, I began to live out my childhood dream of designing women's clothing. As a very young child, I had longed to be a designer; but my low self-image thwarted that dream, since I believed I would never draw or sew well enough. Throughout my youth, though, I plowed through countless fashion magazines, and I sold women's clothing at high-end boutiques in graduate school.

During my time with the birds, it occurred to me that if I could communicate my designs to someone who could sew, I could create anything I wanted. My first dress was a replica from a retro movie that had lived in my head for twenty years. The next garments were entirely my own designs. I never stopped working as a psychologist; I sold my clothing on the side.

As the reader might imagine, many spiritual moments occurred during my design days. For instance, every time I walked next to people sewing on machines or carried bolts of fabric down streets, I felt as though I had done these actions hundreds of times before. This occurred at every fashion production facility I went through—New Mexico, California, New Jersey—and every time I bought fabric. The mundane, rote movements of a designer seemed to be unlocking old, repressed memories. What was going on?

Arthur Funkhouser, PhD, and Harry Perser, PhD, examined déjà vu experiences like mine via the survey method in an eight-year longitudinal study. Their research broke down déjà vu into two distinct subtypes: déjà vécu (already experienced or lived through) and déjà visité (already visited—location based).[39] My experiences would be classified as déjà vecu since they were event-specific and not location-based. As with the research participants in Funkhouser and Perser's study, I too would describe my experiences as "startling," "bewildering," and "precise."[40] The authors discovered that déjà vécu tended to happen more frequently and last longer as compared to déjà visité. Both types of déjà vu, however, were experienced as positive for the study participants, which I also shared.

More bizarre occurrences took place during the development of my clothing line. I worked with two manufacturers at two different production facilities, in two different cities: one produced my cocktail dresses, and the other manufactured my tops. In one of my meetings, the dress manufacturer spontaneously mentioned his family's interpersonal dynamics. "My brother-in-law is horrible," he said. "Everything was great with my sister. We were so close until she married him. He destroyed my family. It's awful."

I was shocked. My manufacturer was going into "session" with me, but he had no idea that I was a licensed psychologist. This man only knew me as a designer. The checks I paid him with listed only my business name. He never knew my last name.

Separately, and shortly thereafter, the second manufacturer echoed a similar occurrence. He grabbed his chest in the middle of a design meeting, "I'm sorry," he said. "My heart keeps beating so fast. It's this anxiety. I've got terrible anxiety. It keeps waking me up at night. It's scary." Again, this man was paid by the same checkbook and did not know my last name. The two men's spontaneous talks were strikingly reminiscent of the three dancers who sought my help inside my freshman dorm. Both men read me, spiritually, just like those dancers had.

As a psychologist, I have helped many clients listen to the Universe and understand the feedback they are being given. The message for me was clear: I may have been a designer in a previous life, but in this lifetime, the Universe wholeheartedly wanted me focused on psychology. Not long after those meetings, I closed my design business.

Throughout my time with the owls and the creation of my clothing line, there was not one day that went by that I did not call my father while he was sick. My claircognizance kept telling me our time together was fading. Every call, every hospital visit, became precious. Yet, there is one day in the hospital that stands out from the others.

While inside his hospital room, mid-chat, he appeared uncharacteristically preoccupied. Something beyond his cancer was invading him, and whatever it was seemed to sour the air. I stopped mid-sentence. "Are you all right, Dad? What is it?"

A gray wash flooded his face, and a solemness found its way to him in a way I had never seen before. Softly, gently, he said, "I feel a need to ask for your forgiveness."

"I already forgave you a long time ago," I said quickly, as if stopping a spill. "It's okay, Dad. Please rest."

Instantly, I knew what had infected the room: shame.

We both understood what my father was referring to. My largest wound—

the idea that I was not smart enough, that there was something wrong with my brain—had been planted by him. Very quickly, we acknowledged the damage. Afraid to worsen his shame, I shut down the talk. He was heart-breakingly awkward and there was nothing more to say.

My father turned to his side and caught a glimpse of life moving outside his hospital window. Soon after, he drifted to sleep. I watched him rest as I might watch a child, feeling protective, hopeful, imagining the vast afterlife ahead of him, and the mysterious connections that brought our family together.

My work with the owls became a second instance of soul recognition. In those animals, I found myself. I met my counterparts. I was no longer alone.

Like an owl, I make my living as a listener. Nearly everything I do pro-fessionally depends on my ability to hear. Just as an owl must hear a vole skittering beneath the soil, I must listen for what is under the surface of what my clients tell me. I hear my clients' unconscious. Their darkness. The location where people hide secrets.[41] And like the winged creature, I, too, am an "extractor of secrets." Highly personal information is what I listen to most of all. And as the owl has been seen as a symbol of death, many of my psychic "hits" concern death.

Athena, Minerva, and Lilith are some of the female warriors whom I cherish. I relate to all the girls and women throughout history who ever refused a life of submission. The wives who see themselves as equal to their husbands. Mighty, independent women who see the Garden of Eden's rules as damnation… Fearsome and efficient, evolved to listen, moving in silence, guided by sound… Putting it all together, I have come to know that I am an owl in human form.

CHAPTER 5

Reincarnation

SUDDEN, OVERWHELMING, STRANGE, AND WARM... THESE ARE THE words I would use to describe my déjà vu feelings as I walked through groups of women huddled over sewing machines in production facilities. Even more, as I shared earlier, the sense that I had done these actions hundreds of times before was consistent across every fashion facility I went through—in multiple US states. Adding to the bizarre quality of my déjà vu was the fact that nothing in my lived, personal history could rightly explain it.

Mystifying episodes like these call into question the possibility of reincarnation. Do these circumstances indicate a person is remembering fragments from a previous life? Stories of déjà vu and past lives have persisted for centuries, and within this assortment of fascinating accounts are reports made by children. Many scholars and laypeople alike find these narratives the most compelling.

In 1961, the Chairman of Psychiatry at the University of Virginia flew halfway across the world to interview children who claimed to recall past lives. This scientist would eventually gather a staggering collection of nearly 3,000 reincarnation cases and travel an average of 55,000 miles per year.[1]

His name was Ian Stevenson, MD, and he would become "the world's most prominent past-life investigator."[2,3] Although formal study in this field began in India in the 1920s,[4] no other researcher, before or since Stevenson, has examined this subject with as much scientific depth and rigor.

Western culture has largely ignored or rejected the idea of reincarnation. But in other parts of the world, especially the Middle East and Asia, belief in reincarnation plays a significant cultural and religious role.[5] Stevenson, however, was never deterred by the West's dismissal; he remained steadfast in his devotion to this subject for fifty years.

Each time Stevenson examined the "survival of personality after death," the pioneer followed his own definition of reincarnation: the idea that people have two separate components—a physical body and a soul. Upon death, then, the soul would persist and become associated with a new physical body.[6]

Like all committed scientists, Stevenson took special care in selecting his research samples. Of utmost importance to him was choosing a group of subjects so worthy of academic study, so rich with powerful evidence, that their details had the potential to quiet the staunchest critics. Keeping this high standard in mind, Stevenson focused heavily on the reports made by children between the ages of two and four.

The academician had a strong rationale for choosing this population: It would be hard to argue that children this young were influenced by culture, religion, or family values. Also, these children were newly born, and their stories of previous lives would, presumably, be fresh in their memories. As well, their current lives were short enough to have been well-documented. Indeed, Stevenson's 300 publications, including fourteen books,[7] were brimming with cases of two-to four-year-old children.

As any astute researcher would, Stevenson saw patterns in his samples. In a seminal text, he gave a description of his average cases. Everything started, Stevenson explained, when a child, usually between the ages of two and four, but occasionally older, began discussing details from a previous life. Many of these children, Stevenson said, started talking about their previous lives as soon as they gained the ability to speak, and sometimes their reports started before they developed good verbal skills. In these scenarios, the child would mispronounce words, and it would be realized later that their botched phrases related to their past life narratives.[8]

Some of the children Stevenson studied made only three or four different statements about their previous lives, but others made as many as sixty or seventy separate statements.[9] Starting around the age of five or six, the child would speak less about their prior life, which suggested to Stevenson that they were starting to forget the details. Usually, by the time the child reached the age of eight, they stopped discussing their previous life entirely.[10]

SPONTANEOUS REPORTS

Any reader of Stevenson's would quickly notice his preference for the word "spontaneous." It was the "spontaneous" nature of the children's reports that cued him to consider a case. The child had to start suddenly discussing a past life without any outside influence. Everything needed to start from there.

METHODOLOGY

Once Stevenson took on a case, he performed an extensive evaluation of the evidence. Critical to his methodology were the following materials: lengthy interviews with the child and their parents, a careful review of the child's medical records (with particular focus on the child's illness history), a medical examination of the child, a close analysis of the autopsy records of the deceased person in question, and an evaluation of the child's artwork. Cases were classified as "solved" when the child's statements, behaviors, and/or physical signs adequately matched the previous personality.

SKEPTICISM

His openness to the concept notwithstanding, throughout his career, Stevenson never stopped being a skeptic. At every step, he considered the possibility that another, alternative explanation might better account for the children's stories. He also considered the possibility of fraud and addressed those rare instances during an interview with the *New York Times,* explaining that, on occasion, a parent would become "intoxicated" by the case's publicity and inflate the story.[11]

As a skeptic, Stevenson also placed greater emphasis on the children's behavioral and/or physical signs of having led past lives, as opposed to their verbal statements, because it is harder for outside influences to affect those pieces of data. Verbal statements, in contrast, can be swayed by psychological and cultural factors. (Such factors would be considered confounding variables, something every researcher aims to eliminate or reduce.)

To Stevenson's delight, there was a plethora of behavioral and physical data for him to forage. Some of Stevenson's most spellbinding cases, roughly 35 percent of them, consisted of children with birthmarks and congenital anomalies that matched the wounds of the deceased persons the children allegedly recalled.[12,13]

In one of his most famous publications, "Birthmarks and Birth Defects Corresponding to Wounds on Deceased Persons," Stevenson reviewed 210 cases and noted how the children's birthmarks were usually hairless, puckered skin with little or no pigmentation, and the birth anomalies were almost always of rare types.[14] Amazingly, in cases where the details of the child's statements matched the deceased person, a close correspondence was usually present between the birthmarks and/or birth anomalies on the child and the wounds on the deceased person.[15] In forty-three of forty-nine cases, for instance, such an overlap was confirmed.[16] Ultimately, Stevenson concluded that some paranormal process must have taken place.

During the aforementioned *New York Times* interview, Stevenson also explained how the birthmarks in these cases were fundamentally different from typical markings: Ordinary birthmarks, he explained, have areas of increased pigmentation and are usually flat, while these birthmarks had decreased pigmentation, scar-like qualities, and tended to be much larger.[17]

Let's dig further into Stevenson's remarkable findings with a little Q & A.

What led Stevenson to conclude that the child's markings and birth anomalies truly matched the deceased personality?

Since Stevenson's work was so controversial, he set exceptionally high standards for confirming that a match had taken place. The overlap of the birthmarks and wounds, on the child and the deceased personality, had to be within ten square centimeters of the same anatomical location.[18]

Some of Stevenson's most remarkable cases involved gunshot wounds. For example, in eighteen cases, the children had two birthmarks—one which corresponded to the entry wound, and another which corresponded to the exit gunshot wound suffered by the previous person.[19] In fourteen of these cases, one birthmark was larger than the other, and in nine of those fourteen cases, the smaller birthmark corresponded to the wound of entry, while the larger, irregular mark matched the exit wound.[20]

Forensic research confirms Stevenson's observations of gunshot wounds, in general. For example, a team of researchers in 2023 explained in their National Institutes of Health ballistics study that exit bullet wounds are usually larger and more irregular than entry gunshot wounds. Entry wounds, the authors explained, show an invagination of tissue, whereas exit wounds tend to have an outward beveling of tissue.[21] One of Stevenson's gunshot cases was a boy who told him that he remembered the life of a man who had been shot in the head from behind. Stevenson's medical photographs of this boy show a small round birthmark on the back of his head and a larger, irregularly shaped birthmark on the front of his head.[22]

Regarding birth anomalies, one case of Stevenson's concerned a girl who was missing her right tibia (shin bone) at birth due to a rare disease known as unilateral hemimelia.[23] According to a 2016 article in the *Journal of Child Orthopedics*, this disease occurs in one of every one million births.[24] What makes this case particularly remarkable is that the girl missing her tibia told Stevenson that she remembered the life of another girl who was killed from being run over by a train. Eyewitnesses from the accident reported that the train first severed the girl's right leg before crushing her.[25]

In general, were the children's markings and birth anomalies related to how the previous personality died?

Yes. Typically, the children's markings and/or congenital anomalies specifically coincided with the fatal wounds suffered by the deceased. Thus, it was not just any physical feature from the deceased that was carried over onto the child's body. It was, arguably, the most identifying mark or physical irregularity—the precise spot that carried the majority of the deceased's physical and psychological pain.

People of all ages have different marks on their bodies. Isn't it possible that the overlap in markings between the child and the deceased personality is simply a coincidence?

When Stevenson addressed this question, he pointed out how the possibility that chance better accounts for the correspondence is greatly reduced when the child has two or more marks that each coincide with the deceased's body. In further exemplifying his point, he described a Thai man with a major abnormality of the skin on the back of his head who, as a child, had recalled the life of his uncle who was stabbed in the head and almost instantly killed. This Thai man also had a deformed toenail that corresponded to a chronic infection his uncle had suffered on the same toe.[26] Readers interested in Stevenson's medical photographs are encouraged to see his 1993 article listed in this book's Notes section.

Did the children in Stevenson's cases have psychological issues that related to the previous personality they claimed to recall?

Yes. More than just physical similarities, Stevenson found the children and the deceased personalities often shared the same phobias, philias (i.e., extreme focus on and fascination with certain objects), illnesses, and special talents and/or unusual behaviors. Amazingly, 36 percent of the children in a series of 387 cases had phobias that specifically related to the mode of death the previous personality endured.[27] In one such case, a girl in Sri Lanka resisted baths so much that, as an infant, three adults had to hold her down just to give her one.[28] Later, when the girl grew older, she also had a profound phobia of buses. She told Stevenson that she remembered the life of another girl who had drowned in flood water when she had stepped back to avoid a bus that drove past her.

James G. Matlock, PhD, is an anthropologist who focuses on reincarnation and near-death experiences. In his research, Matlock describes how the phobias in children with past-life memories do not simply repeat behaviors from the previous personality but rather show the emotional reactions one might expect the previous person would have had, had they lived.[29] For example, one of Matlock's cases of reincarnation concerned a girl who was phobic of thunderstorms and who had a past-life memory of another girl who died during a thunderstorm.

Children's play can be very revealing of their psychological states. Did the children's play activities show any indications of previous lives?

Yes. Beyond phobias, Stevenson also found the children's play tended to match the activities the previous personality engaged in. Specifically, the child's play tended to reenact the previous person's vocation, avocation, or situation of death, which fueled Stevenson's sense that reincarnation may be about continuing "unfinished business" of those whose lives have been cut short by violence, accidents, or illnesses.[30]

How much of the deceased person's lives did the children typically remember?

The children's memories tended to focus most on the last portion of the deceased's life. This nuance is due to the recency effect in memory, according to Matlock.[31] In 1966, Glanzer and Cunitz famously discovered, through repeated experimentation, that people tended to best remember items presented to them last.[32] Matlock explains that this recency effect is why the children's past-life memories predominantly focus on the last year, months, and days of the previous life—why nearly 75 percent of Stevenson's cases accurately described how their previous lives ended.[33]

There are many different types of memory. How do researchers classify the children's memories in Stevenson's cases?

Children with memories of past lives show flashbulb memories. These are highly emotionally charged and spontaneous forms of memory. An example that any American could relate to would be walking along a street, seeing an airplane fly overhead, and then suddenly remembering what one was doing on September 11th, 2001. Flashbulb memories are intense, concern intense subjects, and hit us out of nowhere.

In addition to flashbulb memories, children who report past lives vary to the extent to which they identify with the deceased. Some children insist on being called the previous personality's name and refuse to respond to their given name; others cry or angrily speak of those involved in ending their past lives, and still others use phrases such as "When I was big..." or "I have a wife and two sons."[34]

What is the time period between the death of the previous personality and the child's birth?

Stevenson called this mysterious time period an intermission interval, and he stated it could range anywhere from a few weeks to many years but tended to average around fifteen months.[35] Overall, most of Stevenson's cases had intermission intervals of less than three years.[36]

Prior to his death in 2007, Stevenson founded the Division of Perceptual Studies at the University of Virginia, which remains active today. He appointed psychiatrist Jim Tucker, MD, as its chairman. Tucker worked alongside the legendary researcher for several years and was the lead investigator in one of the most famous cases of reincarnation in the United States. As the reader will now see, the case of James Leininger bears nearly all the hallmarks of Stevenson's illustrious work.

THE CASE OF JAMES LEININGER

James was born to a Protestant couple in California in 1998. At twenty-two months old, his father took him to a flight museum, having no idea how much that one, seemingly routine day might affect his son.

Inside the museum, James was fascinated by the World War II exhibit. His father bought him several toy planes without realizing his son would later smash those same toys repeatedly into the living room furniture while screaming, "Airplane crash on fire!"[37]

Two months later, at two years old, the boy started to have nightmares about plane disasters. "Airplane crash on fire! Little Man can't get out!" James would cry and kick his legs up in the air.[38]

A few months later, the boy told his parents that his nightmares were memories. "My airplane got shot in the engine and it crashed in the water and that's how I died."[39]

James specifically mentioned that his plane was shot by the Japanese and said his airplane was a "Corsair" that flew off a boat called "Natoma." His father searched online and found that the USS Natoma Bay was an aircraft carrier stationed in the Pacific Ocean during World War II.

James's parents repeatedly asked their son about the "Little Man" in his nightmares. The boy said it was either "me" or "James," and he also mentioned a friend named Jack Larsen.

His father then wrote a letter to a World War II veteran who confirmed that Jack Larsen had served on the Natoma Bay. James's father also went to a reunion and discovered that one pilot from the ship was killed: a twenty-one-year-old from Pennsylvania named James M. Huston, Jr.[40]

From the age of three, James began making hundreds of drawings of battle scenes involving airplanes. At four years old, he often signed his art as "James 3." When asked why he wrote three when he was four years old, James explained that the three did not refer to his age, but to his being the third James.[41] James's notion that he was the third may be because the pilot, James Huston, was James, Jr.[42] Shockingly, at six years old, James also told his father how napalm bombs were made.[43]

As a young child, James created a "cockpit" out of an old car seat from inside his father's closet. Repeatedly, James would pretend to be a pilot, tumble out of the closet, and reenact parachuting down to the ground after his plane was shot.

While being interviewed by researchers, James mentioned that Corsairs often had flat tires. This detail was confirmed by historians who reiterated that these WWII planes were notoriously bad in hard landings and regularly got flat tires.[44]

Eventually, it was discovered that Huston's plane crashed exactly where James had described. Researchers closely reviewed the aircraft report for the day that Huston's plane was shot, which showed the flight paths made by each pilot. Jack Larsen was listed as the pilot next to Huston's plane.[45]

James's parents found James Huston, Jr.'s sister, who said the boy correctly identified her and her sister's names. She also said the boy knew things that her brother did as a child.[46]

Ultimately, James and his parents visited Japan and went by boat to the precise location where James Huston Jr.'s plane was shot down. While aboard, the family had a ceremony for the deceased WWII pilot.

I have seen home video footage of this ceremony in which James sobbed throughout. During a later interview, James said that he was able to feel a sense of closure from the onboard memorial service.[47]

Clearly, James's day at the museum of flight as a young child had a profound effect on him. Matlock explains that memories of past lives can be jogged by association with things we see and hear, and he believes that James's experience at the museum triggered his memories.[48]

THE ROLE OF TRAUMA

How a two-year-old child born in 1998 could possibly know the details about planes and pilots from WWII is astonishing. As I read his history, I also imagine how horribly traumatic this must have been for young James to endure. In all those nightmares, toy airplane crashes, and "cockpit" re-enactments, we see a child born with profound emotional pain. We find a baby with a gut-wrenching amount of trauma.

Past-life researchers often cite the work of psychiatrist and trauma specialist Lenore C. Terr, MD. More specifically, they write of a term coined by Terr called "Post-Traumatic Play."[49] According to Terr, children with trauma unconsciously repeat their trauma, symbolically, in their play. And what makes Post-Traumatic Play especially sad is that the child's repeated efforts to understand and process what happened to them ends up making the child feel more anxious. The repetitive play closely resembles the original trauma but fails to resolve the matter, and this cycle is what causes the traumatized child to feel worse.

Given James's level of emotional distress, I have wondered whether he received psychotherapy or medication to help his post-traumatic symptoms.

The answer remains unclear. It is possible, however, that James did receive help and that confidentiality laws prevent me from seeing this information. Notably, Tucker remarked in one of his publications that James was doing well when he met with him again at age seventeen.[50]

It is worth briefly mentioning that Post-Traumatic Play may also occur in situations that are not fully traumatic. In those instances, we simply see that something greatly disturbed the child's developing psyche. For example, as a small child, I saw the movie *The Poseidon Adventure*, in which a cruise ship is pummeled by a massive tidal wave and capsizes. In the movie, the ship's machinery, furniture, and flooring are shown upside down. For years, I would imagine what the room I was sitting in would look like if it were flipped over with the furniture on the ceiling.

THE ROLE OF REPRESSION

One aspect to consider in past-life recall is that, according to the psychoanalytic model, very young children have immature repression barriers (see Chapter 3: Precognitive Dreams). An underdeveloped repression mechanism might help younger children better remember past-life information. Children at this stage would not feel the same unconscious pressure to censor out their memories the way older children and adults would.

WHAT DOES A PSYCHIC MEDIUM THINK OF THESE CHILDREN'S STORIES?

A different perspective on reincarnation comes from psychic medium Meaghan O'Leary, PhD, who has performed hundreds of past-life regressions over the course of more than twenty years. In an interview, I asked O'Leary why she thinks children's reports of past lives are valuable to study:

> *Some of the most compelling case studies we have involve children who are able to recall vivid past life memories, particularly those living in cultures with a belief system that supports reincarnation. In these communities a child is often encouraged to share their impressions which helps to deepen perception. Hundreds of details from these recollections have been verified after researching public records and interviewing friends and family members who knew the person during their previous lifetime. Strong attachments and preferences unrelated to the current life are usually observed, such*

as a different home location, religious practice, language, cuisine or fashion. ... Children are tuned in, psychically, instinctively, and energetically. I believe these states are natural holdovers from our non-physical, spiritual origins and make them especially perceptive to experiences from earlier existences, particularly as newborns and very young children. Reports suggest that by age six or seven, most children are beginning to integrate into the current lifetime and conscious past-life recall diminishes.[51]

ADULT STORIES OF REINCARNATION

Today's parallel to Stevenson is Brian Weiss, MD, former Chairman Emeritus of Psychiatry at the Mount Sinai Medical Center in Miami, Florida. Weiss, more than any other professional in the United States, is the foremost expert on the past lives of adults.

Both esteemed psychiatrists were trained in a mainstream, Western approach. Stevenson earned his medical degree at McGill University, whereas Weiss received his from Yale University. Within their different career trajectories, however, we also see the different specializations within psychiatry; Stevenson focused his research on children, while Weiss has primarily worked as a clinician for adults. Yet, the two pioneers, each with his own stamp, have left an indelible print on the study of reincarnation.

A young woman named Catherine came to see Weiss for help with anxiety, panic attacks, and phobias in the 1980s, and the experience of working with her would permanently change Weiss's life. From his sessions with Catherine, the psychiatrist who once was skeptical of reincarnation would go on to perform thousands of past-life regressions and author several books on the topic—including his most well-known work, *Many Lives, Many Masters,* in which Catherine is featured.

At first, Weiss provided Catherine with conventional psychotherapy. But after eighteen months of seeing only minimal improvements in her debilitating symptoms, Weiss, desperate, tried adding hypnosis into her appointments.

Weiss was shocked by what happened. While in trance, Catherine not only recalled past-life memories that were found to be the causes of her symptoms, but she also communicated with a metaphysical entity called the "Master Spirits" who gave her an array of knowledge about spiritual matters. In one pivotal session, for example, the "Master Spirits" told Catherine highly personal information about Weiss.

From the "Master Spirits," Catherine told Weiss his father's Hebrew name as well as the nature of his father's death. Catherine even knew specifics about Weiss' son, who had died in infancy from a rare heart disease. Catherine's ability to communicate with the "Masters" was startling to Weiss, who explained that his patient was relaying information said to her by this "highly evolved [group of] souls not presently in body."[52]

Over time, Weiss witnessed Catherine become increasingly psychic. During their hypnotic sessions, she started to anticipate Weiss' questions. Many of her dreams also began to have precognitive aspects. Curiously, Weiss noted that, prior to their working together, Catherine had no history of psychic tendencies and held no belief in reincarnation.

Other puzzling instances occurred while Catherine was in trance. For instance, she could quickly move from discussing a memory that took place in antiquity to describing an event that transpired hundreds of years ago, to relaying memories that concerned more recent times. In all, she discussed details from previous lives that spanned thousands of years.

After a few months of hypnosis, Catherine's symptoms of anxiety and depression lifted. Weiss was amazed by what he discovered; his training as a physician did not align with what he was witnessing. Prior to Catherine, he doubted anything that could not be confirmed with traditional scientific methods. Although he knew of parapsychological studies, he had dismissed them all as implausible. In the end, Weiss did not have a scientific explanation for what happened with Catherine.

I had the opportunity to discuss reincarnation further with past-life regressionist O'Leary. In that conversation, she connected the phenomena of past lives with Albert Einstein's First Law of Thermodynamics, which instructs that:

Energy can neither be created nor destroyed, only altered in form.[53]

As I reflected more on Einstein's monumental concept, I wondered whether the man synonymous with the word *genius* ever believed in reincarnation. Throughout my research, I have not found any definitive statements from him. I did, however, discover a rather poignant and revealing autographed letter of Einstein's catalogued by Christie's London auction house.

Not long before his death in 1955, Einstein sent this letter of condolence to the family of one of his closest friends and collaborators, Michele Besso:

Now he has again preceded me a little in parting from this strange world. This has no importance. For people like us, who believe in physics, the separation between past, present and future has only the importance of an admittedly tenacious illusion.[54]

From his letter, it seems Einstein was open to the possibility of reincarnation. Even more, Einstein implied that it was inevitable that he would see Besso again.

When I read Einstein's tender remembrance of his friend, I wondered what the renowned physicist would say about a two-year-old boy who embodied the trauma of a pilot who died more than fifty years earlier. How Einstein might explain the appearance of birthmarks, congenital anomalies, phobias, and philias in children recalling past lives. What Einstein would think about Catherine's past-life memories and her ability to communicate with the "Master Spirits." Her knowledge of Weiss' father's and son's deaths. Her ability to effortlessly dash back and forth between millennia during trance. What would Einstein have to say about all of this?

As I consider the intensity of Defining Moments, I also wonder whether they could be related to or reactions against some sort of past-life matter. People respond to adversity so reflexively during Defining Moments. Big actions are taken instinctively.

Similarly, when I consider how natural it was for me to sit in a counseling role at eighteen in my freshman dormitory, I wonder if something else was going on. Maybe, in addition to being a designer in a former life, I also had another life in which I was a therapist. Perhaps what appeared like a natural ability, with an inherent awareness of confidentiality, was just a reflection of the fact that I had already done the job before.

CHAPTER 6

Synchronicity

His email revealed almost nothing—just his contact information and a desire to start psychotherapy.

"Yes, I am taking new clients," I said, in my email reply. "When would you like to come in?"

And so it was that Qamar entered my life. He did not enter it quietly like my other clients. His appearance was met with great angst—my own. Five years ago, on the morning of Qamar's first appointment, I had a dream in which I was with my deceased father. Dreams of this nature are always shocking. While it is wonderful to see my father again, if only momentarily in a dream, awakening to a reality that no longer includes him is painful. That morning was five years after his death. Today, as I write, it is now ten years since his passing, and my heart feels lighter.

My father rarely appears in my dreams. It has happened only a handful of times since his death. When he does appear, it is only as a silent figure. We communicate telepathically in these dreams, a quality which makes them unusual and especially easy to recall. In this particular dream, my father and I were seated opposite one another in conversation. I cannot remember the specifics of what we discussed, but I remember being totally absorbed.

For this reason, I was completely stunned when, a couple of minutes into his session, Qamar told me that he wanted to start therapy to work on his feelings about his father's death. For a moment, I was speechless. Thankfully, I had conducted many thousands of hours of psychotherapy by that point and could (mostly) hide my shock.

Was my dream precognitive? How did my new client seem to know what was on my mind? Why were we having what seemed like a coincidence? Only two hours before his arrival I was mid-dream with my father. I awoke sad, confused, mournful...

I don't know if Carl Jung would have chuckled or scolded me for my shock and my (almost) sudden case of mutism. One of Jung's greatest gifts to humanity was his theory on these types of strange, seemingly coincidental occurrences. Jung called these incidents "synchronicity"; the term is still alive today, more than ninety years later. But what does *synchronicity* mean? Let's start with the Merriam-Webster dictionary, which defines the term as "the coincidental occurrence of events and especially psychic events that seem related but are not explained by conventional mechanisms of causality."[1]

Jung first wrote about these bizarre, bewildering episodes in the 1930s, and he explored the subject heavily during the last decade of his life. According to Jung, a synchronicity consists of two factors:

> *An unconscious image comes into consciousness either directly (i.e., literally) or indirectly (symbolized or suggested) in the form of a dream, idea, or premonition. An objective situation coincides with this content. The one is as puzzling as the other.*[2]

From my example with Qamar, we see how my dream of my deceased father, a tellingly rare occasion, coincided with an "objective situation"—my client's discussion of his father's death.

The largest influence, by far, on Jung's conceptualization of synchronistic phenomena was Albert Einstein and his theory of relativity. Einstein was Jung's dinner guest on several occasions,[3] and in one of his letters, Jung said it was Einstein who inspired him to think about "a possible relativity of time as well as space, and their psychic [mental] conditionality."[4] Through Jung's endeavor to define synchronicity, he came to see that "in relation to the psyche, space and time are, so to speak, 'elastic' and can apparently be reduced to an almost vanishing point."[5]

And while Jung deepened his understanding of synchronicity, he found it contained an additional Einsteinian subject: energy. Jung saw synchronicity as rooted in a mysterious energy between an individual's mind and their external world.

As Jung mused and chewed over synchronicity, he kept hearing intriguing findings coming out of J.B. Rhine's parapsychological laboratory at Duke University. Rhine had shared with Jung his findings on ESP,[6] which helped Jung see that a part of the psyche must not be subject to the laws of time and space.[7] Eventually, Rhine, the Father of Parapsychology, came to be the second man to influence Jung's notion of synchronicity. And not long after Rhine shared his findings on ESP, Jung would meet another world-renowned scientist who would lead him to further refine his thoughts on synchronistic phenomena. But this person would enter Jung's life in a very different way.

Jung did not release his ideas on synchronicity casually; nor did he do it immediately. He stewed on the mysterious subject for many years. Jung found that when he explored his ideas on the collective unconscious, and theorized that we all have archetypes embedded within our psyches, he kept seeing what appeared like coincidences.[8]

Like my experience with Qamar, Jung also had instances of synchronicities with clients. His most famous synchronistic case concerned a woman reporting a dream in which she was given a golden scarab. While the woman told Jung her dream in his office, a beetle tapped the window next to Jung, who then caught the insect as it flew inside.[9]

Synchronicities, like other parapsychological phenomena, can have additional layers within them. Such was the case with my dream before meeting Qamar. More specifically, my dream contained multiple precognitive components.

First, it could be argued that my dream's main function was one of preparation. By dreaming of my deceased father, I was, in effect, preparing myself to have a session that concerned a very difficult subject. Although the appointment five years ago was focused exclusively on Qamar, that clinical hour was tough on me. My father's death has had such a profound impact on me that I have caught myself counting time by referencing his passing. "Oh, when did X happen? Was that before or after Dad died?"

A second precognitive feature is that Qamar is the only client I have had that has truly reminded me of my father. Thus, my precognition was also preparing my psyche to sit with someone who was like my father. The association of Qamar to my father was so unsettling that it would take me many months before I could consciously see this connection. My initial read on their similarities was strictly unconscious, which is understandable given that Qamar was my twenty-four-year-old psychotherapy client.

Another precognitive aspect of the experience was that in the dream, my father and I were talking while seated across from each other. This physical position is, of course, the same in a psychotherapy session. Well, at least, that was the case when I met Qamar, which was before the 2020 COVID-19 apocalypse and the worldwide Zoom takeover.

In my efforts to understand this synchronicity with Qamar, I have done an emotional audit of sorts. I have looked deep into my memory bank for others who have reminded me of my father—teachers, bosses, friends, camp counselors, professors, therapists, etc. To date, no one has reminded me more of him than Qamar.

Perhaps the largest similarity between these two men is their emotional tone, which helps explain how aspects such as age, race, and religion hold no relevance here. In addition to being young enough to be my son, Qamar is Turkish and was raised in a Muslim family, whereas my father was of Eastern European, Ashkenazi Jewish descent. Their mismatched demographics add further credence to the idea that synchronicities are largely based in energy.

Psychologically, Qamar and my father share numerous qualities; the most salient feature is their strong emotional presence. One of the awful things I have learned as a psychologist is how unusual it is for anyone to have a highly emotionally attuned father. Qamar is arguably the most emotionally attuned male client I have ever worked with. Other shared qualities include their warmth, smile, gentleness, style of laughter, and drive. There is a major piece missing, however, that warrants mention. My father was extremely funny, and although Qamar has a good sense of humor, I would not describe him in this way.

Beyond their shared emotional factors, there are two additional pieces that my rudimentary psychic ability seemed to target: their academic talent and generosity. This is where my sleeping unconscious became startlingly specific with its precognition.

Both my father and Qamar started college early—my father skipped two grades and started university at sixteen. I would not learn of Qamar's early start to college until a year of our work together had passed.

Qamar is also the client I described in Chapter 1, who had the Defining Moment in which he gave away his college scholarship to a financially needier student. I would not learn about this, as well, for a year. Out of the hundreds of clients I have helped, Qamar is the only person who has told me about a Defining Moment that neatly matches the interpretation I provided.

In addition to having started college early, my father shared Qamar's unusual perspective on money. During my high school years, for instance, my father refused to allow my sister or me to apply for scholarships because he believed it would unfairly take money away from financially needy students. My father saw it as unethical for him not to pay for us, not to pay the full freight, when he could afford to send both my sister and me to school. Ultimately, in Qamar's story, we see an academically talented nineteen-year-old with an ethical position on money that precisely replicated my father's attitude.

The fact that a synchronicity could have additional parapsychological components, such as precognitions, illustrates one of the elements that professionals use to criticize parapsychology. Scientists who take this perspective argue that it is problematic for a parapsychological experience to not exist in isolation. Put another way, they see such a multiplicity of components as a discrediting factor: a true parapsychological experience could not be *both* a synchronicity *and* a precognition. In most studies, researchers aim to isolate variables to understand how one factor affects another. Yet, in a somewhat hypocritical manner, these same researchers do not heavily criticize this same crossover problem when it occurs in clinical psychological research.

For example, clients with eating disorders commonly have more than one psychological diagnosis, simultaneously. About half of all patients with eating disorders have some additional psychological diagnosis, such as a mood or anxiety disorder.[10,11] And, very sadly, about a quarter of anorexia patients die by suicide.[12] What these studies consistently show is that researchers *cannot adequately separate* other clinical diagnoses from eating disorder diagnoses. Yet, even with this lack of scientific precision, professionals overwhelmingly agree that eating disorders are an important area of study. So, I wonder, why would this same crossover problem be acceptable for clinical research but unacceptable for paranormal investigations?

Returning to my synchronicity with Qamar, we see Jung's notion of the Father Archetype present for both my client and me. The Father Archetype is one of several archetypes embedded within our collective unconscious that Jung isolated. These archetypes, according to Jungian theory, have existed cross-culturally over thousands of years and repeatedly present themselves in dreams, myths, religions, fairy tales, legends, art, fantasies, and human behaviors. According to Jung, the Father Archetype is an image that belongs to the whole human race and does not simply relate to one person.[13] In fact, Jung theorized that during a synchronicity, psyche and matter connect at an archetypal level of the unconscious.[14]

In my dream, in which I am meeting with my deceased father, who provides me with "wise counsel" telepathically, we see the Father Archetype present. Yet, for Jung, my dream is not just indicative of my actual relationship with my father. Rather, it is more reflective of all father stories and images that have existed since the beginning of civilization, in which a father provides their child with "wise counsel." The Father Archetype is known to represent providers, protectors, wisdom, and "the spirit of the intellect."[15] It is also theorized to appear in situations concerning individualism, self-determination, challenges, battles, and rules.

My conceptualization of a Defining Moment also holds some of the same primordial father energy Jung described for the Father Archetype. During Qamar's Defining Moment, in which he defied the university's rules, he had a direct identification with his father, whom he believes would have been "very proud" of his giving away the scholarship money. Whereas for me, a girl in my Defining Moment, I embodied "the attitude, the spirit by which a man lives"[16] through my willful venturing out into the blizzard. Likewise, when considering the famous examples of Defining Moments I mentioned earlier, it is striking how Gandhi, in his protection of Indian people, came to be known as the "Father of the Nation." All the Defining Moments I have mentioned here, famous or not, seem to hit different aspects of the Father Archetype.

Jung theorized that synchronicities tended to occur in highly emotionally charged situations. His notion echoed the findings of Louisa Rhine, PhD, which determined that precognition happens most during emotionally intense times (see Chapter 3). Even more, Jung theorized that the majority of synchronistic phenomena tended to happen in circumstances involving death, sickness, accidents, risks, and dangers—and often manifested themselves in the forms of precognition, telepathy, and clairvoyance.[17] Certainly, we see the themes of death, telepathy, and precognition in my synchronicity with Qamar.

Yet, there is an additional psychological layer within this one synchronicity that warrants consideration. The fact that I even associated Qamar at all with my father indicates the presence of something called *countertransference*.

Countertransference happens in psychotherapy when the therapist projects their feelings about important people from their past onto their client. In addition to my unconsciously associating Qamar with my father, I have noticed myself feeling highly protective and maternal towards him whenever he describes a situation in which someone has hurt him. This same unconscious, maternal reaction was present when my father mentioned his "need" for my "forgiveness." More specifically, we see a maternal instinct in my efforts not to do anything to worsen my father's shame. Scenarios such as these highlight the messy, irrational nature of feelings. I am not my father's mother, and Qamar is neither my father nor my son. Qamar is my psychotherapy client.

At its core, countertransference is a sign that something within the therapist-client dynamic has deeply affected the therapist. Typically, countertransference occurs when something about the client—it could be their personality, appearance, statements, or behaviors—seems to scratch a therapist's old, unresolved wound(s) in some way. Although countertransference can feel unsettling and even disturbing to therapists, it is not inherently problematic. It is rather a reflection of the very human nature of counseling work and a sign that the professional needs to work on some old issue(s). Two people, with two sets of histories, feelings, relationship patterns, insecurities, traumas, family dynamics, and such, work together to help the client. Countertransference becomes problematic when professionals do not examine their feelings and then inadvertently act out in ways that damage their clients. For a psychologist, "the cost of doing business" is largely emotional. Our clients may (and indeed *should*) stir up feelings within us, but it is our responsibility to work on ourselves constantly.

In my Defining Moment, I unconsciously, and simultaneously, addressed the large wound within myself and identified with my father, the original source of it. Of course, this Defining Moment would also ignite my journey as a psychologist. When examining the dynamics between Qamar and myself, it is easy to see how a man similar to my father would both hit the wound and give me an opportunity to heal any remaining damage from it. It is my intelligence, education, and training that enable me to help Qamar. As a man who emotionally resembles my father, Qamar's personality and character helped my mind unconsciously react to him as the perfect countertransferential object. Other clients who bear no likeness to my father cannot do this. Welcome to the lovely, intense world of psychotherapy! All of us have wounds, but psychotherapy requires us to work on those issues.

Jung noted that synchronicities, and other parapsychological phenomena between therapists and clients, tended to happen when there was some type of transference present within the therapeutic dynamic. In one instance, Jung was traveling for a lecture and woke up in the middle of the night in his hotel room with a terrible headache. He also felt as though someone had entered his room and even got up and looked out into the hallway to check whether anyone was present. The next day, Jung received a telegram stating that his client had ended his life by suicide and that he had shot himself in the head. Jung considered the incident to be synchronistic and further explained that it involved an archetypal situation: death.

As Jung stated of this event,

> *By means of a relativization of time and space in the unconscious it could well be that I had perceived something which in reality was taking place elsewhere...*

> *In this case the unconscious had knowledge of my patient's condition. All the evening, in fact, I had felt curiously restive and nervous, very much in contrast to my usual mood.*[18]

Brian Weiss also described synchronistic phenomena between himself and his patient, Catherine. In one instance, he suddenly woke from a deep sleep and had a larger-than-life-sized image of Catherine's face looking at him, pleading for help. The next day, he learned that Catherine had awakened from a nightmare at that same time, in a state of panic. Weiss explained that both he and Catherine were becoming increasingly psychic. Each of them had developed some ability to communicate telepathically with the other.[19]

The alchemical mixture between a clinician and their client would be the very thing that helped Jung refine his groundbreaking ideas on synchronicity. This extraordinary pairing began in 1932 when the physicist, Wolfgang Pauli, PhD reached out to the famed psychiatrist for help.

At the time, Pauli was a well-established Austrian physicist with a thriving academic career. Eventually, however, over a little more than a decade, his professional status would skyrocket—Pauli would win the Nobel Prize in Physics (an award that Einstein nominated him for) and would be forever known as one of quantum physics' greatest pioneers. Of all his academic accomplishments, Pauli is most known for the exclusion principle, or Pauli principle, which states that "no two electrons in the same atom can have identical values for all four of their quantum numbers."[20]

Pauli was in a terrible state when he contacted Jung: his mother had recently died by suicide; his father had married a woman who was Pauli's age; Pauli's own marriage had just ended; and he was drinking excessively.[21] At his father's prompting, Pauli contacted Jung for psychotherapy.

There is considerable debate over the extent to which Pauli was directly analyzed by Jung. What is known for certain is that Jung initially recommended that Pauli work with one of his colleagues, Jungian analyst Erna Rosenbaum. Some argue that Pauli stayed with Rosenbaum for the remainder of his therapy, and that Rosenbaum recorded Pauli's dreams, which Jung analyzed separately. Others state that Pauli only worked with Rosenbaum for a few months and then switched over to being Jung's client.

Regardless of the specifics, it was Jung's exploration of Pauli's dreamlife that most helped Pauli see the depth and significance of the unconscious. Throughout their work together, Pauli shared approximately 1,300 of his dreams with Jung.[22]

Jung classified dreams according to two major categories:

1.—"Little Dreams," which stem from our personal unconscious and are based on our specific life circumstances. These dreams often contain the residue of our thoughts and feelings from the same day.

2.—"Big Dreams" that originate from deeper layers within the psyche. Dreams of this nature contain the material from the collective unconscious—the thoughts, feelings, and archetypes shared by all people. Jung was, overwhelmingly, more interested in "Big Dreams," and soon into his work with Pauli, he saw the scientist tended to have dreams of this nature. Two "Big Dreams" that have been discussed in this book are my Father Archetypal dream prior to meeting Qamar, and Lincoln's precognitive dream which concerned the archetypal situation of death.

Several months after Pauli ended his psychotherapy, he wrote Jung a letter about a dream he had in which he saw a connection between physics and psychology. Pauli did not know that Jung had already been stewing on synchronicity for years at that point. Pauli's note sparked a letter exchange between the two men that would last several years, and it was through their letter correspondence that Jung would come to deepen his understanding of synchronicity.

Today, therapists and clients, and even former therapists and clients, are forbidden to work together outside of therapy. Doing so is considered a dual relationship and an ethical violation. But in Jung's time, no one would have taken issue with his actions.

Setting aside ethical questions, there was a critical letter exchange between the two men that helped Jung most clearly understand synchronicity. Jung sent Pauli a diagram of his thoughts, and Pauli critiqued Jung's image by explaining to him that he had wrongfully placed time and space as opposite of one another. Pauli reminded Jung of Einstein's monumental discovery that time and space were not opposites—they were intrinsically linked.[23] He strongly encouraged Jung to alter his diagram, so that space and time could be placed along a single continuum.[24]

Through tweaks such as this, back and forth, Jung came to clarify his theory on synchronicity. During this period, Pauli also shared with Jung mathematically expressed ideas on the topic and further suggested to him that he broaden the notion of archetypes to include probability.[25] In general, Jung, who was tortured by math in his youth, felt overwhelmed but highly appreciative of Pauli's mathematical insights.[26,27]

Beyond synchronicity and archetypes, Pauli shared other compelling ideas on Jungian theories. In his letters to Jung, for instance, he made analogies between the atomic nucleus and Jung's construct of the Self, and he connected Jung's theory of the mandala (a circle that represents the wholeness of the Self) with the structure of the heart.[28] For instance, Pauli saw the four-fold aspect of the heart as evidence that physical evolution was also directed toward the goal of completeness.[29] Four-fold images and structures were of special interest to Jung. He called images that were presented in this manner "quaternities." For Jung, the quaternity is an image that represents wholeness, and the mandala is one such example.

In all, Jung and Pauli's professional relationship lasted twenty-six years. Jung formally launched the C.G. Jung Institute in 1948, with Pauli as one of its founding members. The two colossal theorists continued to correspond by letter and publish on synchronicity until Pauli's death in 1958.

The fact that Jung drew into his life a physicist of Pauli's caliber is particularly intriguing. Pauli had such a profound understanding of Einstein's work that he dazzled Einstein himself. During his youth, Pauli captured the preeminent physicist's attention and respect when he published an article on the theory of relativity. Einstein wrote,

Whoever studies this mature and grandly conceived work might not believe that its author is a twenty-one-year-old man. One wonders what to admire most, the psychological understanding for the development of ideas, the sureness of mathematical deduction, the profound physical insight, the capacity for lucid, systematical presentation, the knowledge of the literature, the complete treatment of the subject matter, or the sureness of critical appraisal.[30]

Somehow, Jung had attracted a physicist with the highest level of understanding on the exact theory most connected with synchronicity. Was Jung's relationship with Pauli somehow part of a scheme in the Universe? Could it be that their meeting had been preordained in some way?

Recently, I had a synchronicity with another client that had a very different quality than my synchronicity with Qamar. My client, Matt, told me that he wanted to live with his girlfriend of eight months and had sifted through various real estate listings. One night at dinner, his girlfriend spontaneously mentioned the possibility of their cohabitating and showed him photos of apartments she had pulled off the internet. They were the same photographs Matt had previously saved. Even more remarkable is the fact that the couple had never discussed the possibility of living together until that dinner.

As Matt laughed throughout his story, I told him that he and his girlfriend had a synchronicity. Matt works in finance and was, understandably, not familiar with this psychological term. While I explained it, I held back from telling Matt that his story had a second synchronicity. Just minutes before his session, I was writing this chapter on synchronicity and those fresh sentences were sitting inside my computer less than ten feet away from him. I told Matt about the meta, synchronicity-within-a-synchronicity during a later appointment, and we had a good laugh about it.

Above all, through his explorations on synchronicity, Jung saw these types of seemingly random, "chance" events as:

'coincidences' which were connected so meaningfully that their 'chance' concurrence would represent a degree of improbability that would have to be expressed by an astronomical figure.[31]

Beyond psychotherapy and physics, the theory of synchronicity has been linked to religion, spirituality, esotericism, philosophy, mythology, politics, and shamanism. Jungian scholar and professor Roderick Main, PhD, tells us that synchronicity represents the culmination of Jung's lifelong exploration of the paranormal.[32]

In considering Jung's connections with some of the greatest minds of the twentieth century, I am thinking of the loneliness Jung faced in his childhood. How he longed to have intellectually stimulating conversations in his youth—not just with his father, but with other children and adults, anyone who might welcome his questions. Jung once remarked that, even at home, he never heard anyone discuss intellectual topics.[33]

During his adulthood, Jung addressed those old feelings of isolation. With Freud, Einstein, and Pauli, he could sit and speak with thinkers—men who were questioners, by nature. Men who took pleasure in twisting, breaking, and creating ideas. Men who played with thoughts the way boys played with toys and balls. Instinctively, Jung knew the pain he felt from his early days could only be remedied by intellectuals. As Jung is thought to have said, "We don't get wounded alone and we don't heal alone."

CHAPTER 7

Premonitions

ABRAHAM LINCOLN KNEW HE WAS DESTINED FOR GREATNESS AND disaster. It plagued him. Haunted him. Nothing could stop his grim awareness of his tragically mixed fate.

In 1872, Lincoln's biographer, Ward Hill Lamon, described the sixteenth president of the United States as:

> *The saddest man of his time [with] gloomy forebodings of impending evil, mingled with extravagant visions of personal grandeur and power ... gilded with glory yet tarnished with blood. It was his 'destiny'. ... He never doubted for a moment but that he was formed for 'some great or miserable end.' He talked about it frequently and sometimes calmly. ... It took the character of a 'religious conviction.' ... To him it was fate, and there was no escape or defense. The presentiment never deserted him: it was clear, as perfect, as certain, as any image conveyed by the senses. ... All doubts had faded away, and he submitted humbly to a power which he could neither comprehend nor resist. ... The star under which he was born was at once brilliant*

*and malignant: the horoscope was cast, fixed, irreversible, and he
had no ... power to alter ... it.*[1]

I have had a few premonitions throughout my life, but unlike Lincoln,
none of mine ever involved greatness. However, one of my premonitions
was especially tragic. It was the awareness that the woman who named
me, birthed me, raised me, loved me, and feared for me on the day of my
audition would soon be leaving this Earth.

It was seven months after my father died, and my mother had not yet
settled into widowhood. I remember where I was sitting as I spoke with
her on the telephone one day. My "owl ear" heard that her voice was off.
She said it was allergies. I felt it was something else.

Some part of me knew right then that I would never hear my mother's
real voice again. Not in the way she truly sounded. A part of me knew on
that day that she was already gone.

My rational mind worked hard to quiet my intuition. Perhaps her
allergies *were* awful? Climate change was a thing. Maybe I was being
extreme. Dramatic. I tried my best to explain away my feelings, but
nothing could stop the current of dread that flowed steadily within me
from that moment.

Soon thereafter, she mentioned something strange. She woke one morning on her living room couch with the front door standing wide open. So
exhausted the day before, she had fallen asleep for many hours, never waking
to eat. "Wasn't that funny?" she said.

Months later, I received an email from her that looked odd. Littered with
spelling and grammatical mistakes, it was not the note of a strong writer,
which I'd always known her to be. Just then, my mind shifted to a day we
saw psychological tests in graduate school. One of the testing protocols we
reviewed included a writing sample that contained a huge number of spelling and grammatical errors. The professor said the writing sample showed
organicity. Signs of brain damage. *Organicity.* A word I never imagined
could apply to my mother.

I begged her to have a brain scan. "I'm just having a hard time without
your father," she said. "I think that's all it is. Please, you're making me anxious. I don't need this right now."

Not long after, a security guard had to be called to take my mother home.
She was lost in the neighborhood and frightened.

Then, there was a call about a car accident. Her crash was minor, but the doctor found a cancerous tumor that had been growing inside her brain for more than a year. It was the tumor, he said, that changed her voice.

She agreed to surgery but declined further treatment. The doctor said there were only months left. "I have lived a good life with your father, you and your sister, and the grandchildren. I'm ready to die," she told me.

My mother's acceptance of death swiftly morphed into obsession. She was always a woman in control and now, with the largest, most uncontrollable human experience looming ahead, she desperately needed to harpoon it. Drag it. Take it down on her terms.

She moved back to New York, where my sister oversaw her care. I visited her repeatedly, but after one of my trips, and the moment I was back home, my heart would not stop racing and my stomach could not settle. Quickly, my mother's condition consumed my every thought except for when I was with clients. With them, I could be present. I could pivot toward them. I could get absorbed in their stories, and for fifty-minute stretches of time, I could focus on someone other than my mother.

But each day after my trip, my feelings grew worse. What was once anxiety became panic. Psychological techniques and medications turned useless. There was no sleep for more than a couple of hours a night; I could not eat. Soon, I began to run a fever.

So unrelenting, so horrible was this sense of doom that swelled inside me. It was constant, as the tide speaks with the moon. Nothing could hold it back. It could not be beaten.

I called my sister and then a family friend. Each tried to console me: "She's fine. Nothing has changed." After the calls, I would lie down on my bed.

I tried to rest; it had been five days of misery since I last saw my mother on that trip. But my terrible feelings still would not stop. Curled up on my side, with my eyes closed, the voice of an elderly man spoke into my left ear. "Go to New York," he sternly instructed. The hairs on my body stood on end and stayed stiff like good soldiers. This man was a guide, I thought. Even more, he felt familiar.

Refusing to believe my mother was "fine," I booked a flight and packed a bag. My client sessions for that week were finished, and I was clear to leave. That same decisive, *I don't give a crap about a goddamned blizzard* attitude ignited. Full throttle.

The next day, in the middle of my relief at arriving back in New York, I was forcibly struck by how puzzled my mother appeared as she stood hunched over her walker. The cancer made her unsteady, but long before her brain had been taken by disease, she had often feared falling.

"Davis, you were just here. It's nice to see you, but what's going on?"

"You called me."

"No. I didn't call you. I haven't called anyone for a few days."

"You didn't call me on the telephone, Mom. It wasn't like that. It was different."

She went still. Then she turned away from me and back again. She angled toward me with her hunched body. A brightness came upon her face, and I could see a joy within her work its way throughout her entire being. The lightness I had not seen inside her since before my father fell sick had returned. Right then, intuitively, my mother sensed that her salvation was coming, however it looked to her. What she had longed for most of all was imminent.

"Is it happening?" she asked with great intensity, and there was no question what "it" meant.

"Yes, Mom. It's starting to happen. That's why you called me." The tears streamed down my face.

"You're a witch!" my mother laughed.

I laughed and cried at once. "I don't know about that."

"Can you make it happen faster?" My mother laughed again.

Laughing and crying harder now, I responded, "No, Mom. I love you. Sorry. I'm not here to kill you."

Within hours, my mother's wish started to come true. Later that day, we took her by ambulance to the hospital.

On the last night she spoke to me, she rocked her body back and forth in her bed with her eyes closed. To my shock, she began to speak in a foreign language I could not identify. Speaking, pausing, speaking. I noticed a rhythm to her words. My mother, it seemed, was in a conversation with someone or something I could not see or hear.

Suddenly, she stopped and opened her eyes. "What's happening? I'm so confused," she asked.

"You're between the worlds," I told her. "A part of you is with me and a part of you isn't."

"Am I dying? Is it happening?"

"Yes, Mom. You're dying," I held her hand.

She closed her eyes and spoke again in the foreign language. Then, once more, she opened her eyes and stared straight into me, right through me, into the back of my being, and said, "You're the Gatekeeper."

She closed her eyes again and said something more in the other language. Within a moment, she stopped speaking. She went into a coma and died two days later.

Spiritual writers tell us that the Owl is the Gatekeeper to other realms. The bird, they say, is a symbolic guide between this world and the afterlife. My mother would never have known about the spiritual significance of owls. Neither of my parents had any interest in spirituality or the paranormal. Neither one of them even believed in the idea of a soul. But I think my mother saw me on a spirit level that night.

Not long after, I tried to identify the language my mother was speaking. My first thought was Aramaic, one of the world's most ancient languages, but after watching videos, I ruled it out—as well as Hebrew, Latin, and Greek. The language she spoke also did not resemble any of the Germanic, African, romance, Slavic, or Asian languages I have heard. To this day, the language remains a mystery.

Many have described the words of dying people as "gibberish." Similarly, Jung pointed out how the language of schizophrenics often was considered "meaningless."[2] But the words of the dying did not seem like babble to me. Nor do the jumbled phrases of psychotics. It is amazing how much people fear and readily dismiss whatever they do not understand.

My mother's speaking this foreign language is an example of *xenoglossy*, which was first coined as a term in 1905 by Charles Robert Richet, who would later receive the Nobel Prize for Physiology or Medicine in 1913 for his work on anaphylaxis.[3,4] Brian Weiss also talks about xenoglossy and defines it as the ability of someone to speak a foreign language to which they have never been exposed.[5] James Matlock writes that Ian Stevenson observed xenoglossy in some reincarnation cases and categorized it as either:

- reactive xenoglossy, in which someone uses an unknown language in an automatic, non-comprehending capacity.

- responsive xenoglossy, whereby the person understands and speaks intelligibly in an unlearned language.[6]

My hearing the elderly man, who told me to go to New York to see my mother, is an example of *clairaudience*. Out of all my psi abilities, clairaudience has been the least present and the last to develop for me. Very rarely have I been clairaudient. Yet, because of the intensity of my premonition, and the extreme situation of my mother's impending death, this typically dormant psi ability became activated—an experience consistent with Rhines' and Jung's observations.

Hearing the voice was scary, at first. I knew the voice was not my inner monologue and sensed it came from somewhere else. But how did I know this was not an auditory hallucination?

Let us imagine, for a moment, that I reported at a medical clinic, "A strange man spoke into my ear and told me to do something," but I gave no context, and no one asked me for details. Although these raw facts are true, we can see how different my situation might appear to the listener and how such a sparse rendition of my story might affect how I was interpreted, clinically. Whenever the possibility of psi presents itself, mental health professionals need to know the full story to adequately assess the scenario. Psychiatrists and psychologists who are not at least open-minded about the possibility of the paranormal will not be able to distinguish psychopathological from parapsychological.[7] Everything would be interpreted as mental disturbance.

One group of people who do have auditory hallucinations are schizophrenics. Recent studies published by the National Institutes of Health indicate that 60–80 percent of these patients have this symptom.[8,9] Considering these statistics, how could a clinician in this hypothetical scenario be certain that I was not having a schizophrenic episode with an auditory hallucination?

Whenever I think diagnostically, I look for what symptoms are present, but I also consider which factors are missing. Very often, the absent pieces are far more telling, psychologically.

First, let's consider the specifics of the voice itself, which was a command from an elderly man. When schizophrenics have command hallucinations, the instructions range anywhere from neutral to harmful (toward themselves and/or others). The voice I heard, in contrast, was neither neutral nor harmful. Its command was helpful, and it was immediately interpreted by me as supportive. Also, critical to understanding the diagnostic picture is the location of the voice. I only heard the voice in my left ear, and I felt as though it was coming from within my own head. Schizophrenics typically hear voices in both ears, simultaneously (in stereo), and they sometimes believe the voice is coming from outside of their heads.

In essence, schizophrenia is a thought disorder. During the time I heard the voice, there were no changes in my thinking. I showed no signs of paranoid ideation, such as believing other people were trying to harm me. I also had no difficulty understanding people. I went to work every day, and I focused on my clients. Although no one formally evaluated me with a mental status examination, I could have easily relayed the date, my location, who the president was at that time, etc. Overall, there were no indications that my thinking or my basic mental orientation were disrupted.

Another piece noticeably absent was something called a prodromal period. Schizophrenics commonly have a phase of time, usually lasting several months, in which they steadily, psychologically decline. Throughout this period, they often become asocial and apathetic, and may stop engaging in self-care like bathing and brushing their teeth. Schizophrenics may also stop dressing appropriately for the weather and situation during this period. I was exhibiting none of these behaviors.

Other important pieces missing from my psychiatric presentation were emotional signs of major psychopathology. For example, I did not have a flattened or inappropriate affect. A flattened affect occurs when someone shows no facial expressions while speaking, and an example of an inappropriate affect would be laughing hysterically during a funeral. My mood was low, which was appropriate to the situation. I was neither irritable nor lethargic, states which commonly occur with severe mental illness.

I had a few notable clinical symptoms—extreme anxiety, insomnia, and lack of appetite—but all were explainable by my concern for my mother. Considering, diagnostically, the factors that indicate a severe mental disturbance, there is no evidence that I was suffering from major psychopathology. Voices heard by schizophrenics happen within a clinical context. In those situations, we see a constellation of other debilitating symptoms happening around the same time that the voice or voices appear. What we see in my case is a psychiatrically normal person who heard a voice.

The research team of Powers et al., (2017) from Yale University, published a study that compared clairaudient psychics with schizophrenics. Major differences were found between these two groups. For instance, the patients with schizophrenia reported that they often felt tortured by the voices they heard, whereas the psychics were far more likely to experience the voices as benevolent and helpful. Another critical difference was the age of onset of hearing voices. Clairaudient psychics were found to have an average age of first hearing voices at seven and a half years old—far younger than the schizophrenic group, who had an average age of onset of hearing voices at 22.9 years.[10] The researchers also found that, unlike schizophrenics who were passive receivers of verbal information, the clairaudient psychics regularly sought out the voices. Moreover, the psychic group had an ability to control the voices: "I can turn things on and turn things off. When I'm working, I open myself and when I'm not, I turn it off, like a switch," one psychic explained.[11] Another clairaudient psychic told the researchers, "I say it out loud. 'I'm off duty now. Go away!'"[12]

The professional clairaudient psychics from Powers et al. (2017) are comfortable hearing voices as compared to my own initial, fearful response. And yet, when we consider that I only became clairaudient at thirty-nine years old, it is easy to see why I would react this way. My other psi abilities—claircognizance, clairsentience, clairvoyance, precognition, etc.—began in childhood. Such a difference in the professional clairaudient psychics and myself underscores the degree to which psi abilities exist on a continuum (see Chapter 2). More specifically, my example demonstrates the differences between an amateur with many psi episodes and a professional psychic.

Living with psi is not always easy. Through the different intuitive channels, we can learn emotionally difficult information—things anyone, any rational person, would prefer to ignore. But never was I more thankful for being wired the way I am than with my mother's situation. My "owl ear" knew something was terribly wrong, and my intuition, with its psychic tendencies, prepared me for her illness and brought me to her.

I have never been able to identify the male voice I heard that day. Whoever he was, I am deeply grateful for him. He protected me—and, by extension, my mother. The voice sent me to her when she needed me most. Perhaps he was an ancestor. There was a sense of familiarity to his voice. But perhaps I am wrong, and we share no blood. Regardless of who he was, his mission was clear. He was there for love.

CHAPTER 8

Near-Death Experiences

PSYCHIATRIST ELIZABETH KÜBLER-ROSS TACKLED WHAT MAY BE THE most taboo subject of all—death—with her groundbreaking, international bestselling book, *On Death and Dying*. In this 1969 work, Kübler-Ross identified five stages of grief—denial, anger, bargaining, depression, and acceptance—outlining the path we face in our final days.

As a pioneer in thanatology, the scientific study of death, Kübler-Ross inspired scores of physicians and researchers. One of the people she greatly affected was Raymond Moody, Jr., MD, PhD—a psychiatrist and philosopher working on his own death-centered bestseller.

Unlike Kübler-Ross, who focused on the emotional aspects of death and dying, Moody's book zeroed in on *the literal process of dying*, which made his work especially taboo.

So, how did Moody demystify life's most enigmatic event in his 1975 book, *Life After Life*? He investigated *how* we die by studying patients who had *almost* died.

As Moody learned more and more about these people's transcendental encounters with death, he called their episodes near-death experiences (NDEs)—a term he personally coined. The NDE is defined as a series of profound events that occur while someone is close to dying and often in-volves the ceasing of brain wave activity or cardiac arrest.

Moody knew the characteristics of his sample would be critical to the credibility of his discoveries. Hoping to extend his findings to the population at large, Moody collected a group of cases who best represented the general American public. For more than a decade, Moody studied and interviewed 150 patients from different religious, cultural, educational, and economic backgrounds, all of whom had nearly died.

What shocked readers most and made Moody's work so compelling was not the volume of diverse cases with NDEs that made up his study; instead, it was the *patterns* in what he discovered. It was the *similarities* across the various people's stories that stunned.

Although Moody's book captivated readers, he was not the first physician to report phenomena of this nature. Reports like these have appeared in medical literature since 1740, when a military doctor from northern France, Pierre-Jean du Monchaux, described a patient who had an excessive amount of blood drawn to treat a fever and almost died from the procedure—but came back.[1] What made Moody different—what made his work a landmark study—was that he was the first person in modern times to examine NDEs from a *systematic perspective*.[2]

Not long after Moody's book debuted, other researchers, such as Ian Stevenson and Kenneth Ring, PhD (Professor Emeritus at the University of Connecticut), began studying NDEs in greater detail. These scientists wanted to examine Moody's patterns, and they wanted to understand NDEs through large statistical datasets. Thus, what began with Moody's qualitative case reports grew into a flurry of all-out NDE quantitative investigations. Eventually, so much interest in the field blossomed that a scholarly, peer-reviewed journal was created in 1981, *The Journal of Near-Death Studies,* which states that no scientific explanations thus far have fully accounted for these kinds of events.[3]

In my review of the literature, I have delved into the question of how often these fascinating episodes happen and have only found rough estimations. Jefferey Long, MD, a radiation oncologist and researcher who started the Near-Death Experience Research Foundation, states that NDEs are reported by approximately 17 percent of people who almost die.[4] A Dutch study pub-lished in the medical journal *Lancet* found a rather similar percentage. The authors of that study discovered that 18 percent of 344 cardiac patients who were successfully resuscitated reported NDEs.[5] Professor Bruce Greyson, MD, Emeritus of Psychiatry and Neurobehavioral Sciences at the University of Virginia School of Medicine, states that over nine million people in the United States have reported NDEs.[6]

Given how horribly traumatic it may be for someone to come close to death, it is possible that the actual number of NDEs is substantially higher than reported. Many people may psychologically block out and, understandably, repress an NDE. Also, the number of patients saved from the brink of death may be much larger today because of medical advances.

However, returning to Moody, it is important to note that he *did* find qualitative differences in the episodes that people shared with him. For instance, he found that patients with an actual, clinical death who died for longer periods of time detailed "more florid, complete experiences" than those who only came close to death.[7] Also, Moody found fifteen separate elements that people described in their NDEs. In reviewing Moody's elements, Greyson found that no two NDE accounts were precisely the same, no one element appeared in every narrative, no one experience included more than twelve of these fifteen elements, and the order in which these elements appeared varied among cases.[8] After his book was released, Moody further stated that his list was neither fixed nor exhaustive.[9]

Below are the fifteen elements identified by Moody, listed precisely in the categories he specified. I have also included other findings from different researchers who specifically examined Moody's claims:

INEFFABILITY

Moody found that most people struggled to express their experiences verbally, regardless of a prior proclivity toward verbal description. As one participant stated, "They just don't make adjectives and superlatives to describe this."[10]

HEARING THE NEWS

The dying person typically remembered hearing the doctor or others around them pronounce them dead. One woman in Moody's case file, for instance, heard her doctor say to a second doctor, "Let's try one more time and then we'll give up."[11]

FEELINGS OF PEACE AND QUIET

Moody's cases overwhelmingly reported feelings of peace and quiet and freedom from pain. Other researchers have found that 60–88 percent of people with NDEs describe this same sense of peace.[12,13,14]

THE NOISE
Some of Moody's cases reported hearing unusual and even unpleasant sounds occurring at or near death. One man described a "bad buzzing noise coming from inside [his] head."[15]

THE DARK TUNNEL
Many people told Moody they went through some sort of dark space that was similar to a tunnel, a cave, a well, a trough, an enclosure, a vacuum, a void, a sewer, and a cylinder.[16] Other studies have found that over half of NDE cases describe this same type of passage through darkness.[17]

OUT OF BODY EXPERIENCE
The participants in Moody's study tended to find themselves looking at their own bodies from a spectator's vantage point. They often felt as if they were watching themselves on a stage and described a floating, weightless, drifting sensation.[18] A group of researchers found that more than a third of their sample had this same type of out of body experience.[19] Weiss also writes of how people with NDEs may feel detached from their bodies and watch resuscitation efforts from high above.[20]

MEETING OTHERS
Many people in Moody's sample became aware of the presence of other spiritual beings during their transition state. These beings were there either to help ease the process or to directly tell the patient that it was not their time to die.[21] Other researchers report that roughly 40–64 percent of people with NDEs have this same type of meeting.[22,23]

THE BEING OF LIGHT
Out of all the elements Moody isolated, he states that it is the interaction with a "being of light" that tends to have the strongest emotional impact on the dying person. Many in Moody's sample described this light as loving, warm, and accepting and said they felt a magnetic attraction toward it. Nearly three-quarters of people with NDEs in other studies have also reported to researchers a similar encounter with this "brilliant" light.[24,25,26]

THE REVIEW

Moody and other researchers have found that people with NDEs are given an extraordinarily rapid review of their life experiences.[27,28] One woman described how the ball of light guided her through her life review:

> The things that flashed back came in the order of my life, and they were so vivid. The scenes were just like you walked outside and saw them, completely three-dimensional, and in color. ... I saw myself doing things, as a child. ... All through this, [the light] kept stressing the importance of love. ... [The light] seemed very interested in ... knowledge [and] kept pointing out things that had to do with learning....[29]

THE BORDER OR LIMIT

Some demarcation was commonly described to Moody by his sample. This border presented itself in different permutations such as a body of water, a door, a section of mist, or a fence across a field.[30] One participant said:

> I felt certain that I was going through that mist.... Yet, it wasn't my time to go through the mist, because instantly from the other side appeared my Uncle Carl, who had died many years earlier. He blocked my path, saying, "Go back. Your work on Earth has not been completed. Go back now.[31]

Other researchers have found that nearly one quarter of NDE cases describe this type of border.[32]

COMING BACK

In many of Moody's cases, the dying person did not want to come back to life and resisted the return into their body. Another researcher found this same resistance in 36 percent of their NDE cases.[33]

TELLING OTHERS

Understandably, many participants told Moody that they had resisted the urge to tell people their stories out of fear that they would be judged mentally unstable.

EFFECT ON LIVES

Most people in Moody's sample felt their lives were enriched by the experience—so much so that it prompted them to change their attitudes about life and death. In general, Moody's sample became more reflective and developed a stronger interest in philosophical issues as a result of their NDE.

NEW VIEWS OF DEATH

"Almost every person" told Moody they "no longer" feared death as a result of their NDE.[34]

CORROBORATION

Doctors were overwhelmingly puzzled by how well Moody's cases were able to describe in detail the procedures that were used for their resuscitations.

Although the other researchers strategically examined Moody's fifteen themes, they did not discuss their NDE cases in detail. Almost all these authors presented statistical datasets. After reading Moody's work, I wanted to explore more cases of NDEs in depth. Specifically, I wanted to see if I could find within the academic literature NDE cases that showed Moody's elements. I wanted to see if I could find an overlap between Moody's results and NDE cases that were never studied by him. My findings were astonishing.

CASE #1

In 2014, the *Missouri Medicine* journal published an article written by physician Jean Renee Hausheer, MD, who described how she almost died at the age of twenty. Within her article, Hausheer details her own NDE and its dramatic effect on her.

As a medical student, Hausheer suddenly developed symptoms of double vision and went to the emergency room.

At the hospital, her neurological symptoms worsened, causing her to have difficulty breathing. Her doctor then inadvertently gave her a medication that further worsened her breathing, sending young Jean Renee into acute respiratory failure:

I saw, as if from above and apart, like watching a television drama, emergency resuscitation efforts ... I viewed the frenetic activities around my dying body with detached interest. ... Ahead emerged a wondrous, brilliant ball of the unimaginably whitest light from which emanated perfect love and peacefulness. Despite its infinite luminosity, the light was pleasing and caused my eyes no discomfort. ...

As I departed, there was never recognition that what lay below was my dying body. It was not a part of me, and the surrounding medical drama was not my concern. ...

This radiant ball of loving light initially appeared at a distance and rapidly surrounded my soul during my journey. The light sourced from a beautiful central ball-like brilliance ... this ... transcendent light was a peaceful, living, loving thing ... pure love and acceptance. ... Very naturally and effortlessly, I was drawn to this living ball of loving light. ... The love source and my soul merged within the light. ... It was a welcoming home, as if the loving light source was now whole again, and so was I. ... The process halted. ... A voice spoke to me. The voice wasn't male or female, was audible and came from within this amazing living ball of lighted love. The voice surrounded me ... [and] said ... "Don't worry. It's not your time yet. Return!"

I suddenly awoke on a respirator in the intensive care unit ... I could see and hear all these people ... trying to save me. ... I knew I was going to survive. ...

Once I got my hands on pen and paper, I wrote out an explanation ... of my near-death experience. ... I knew I was going to be fine ... Now was not my time to die. ... I was at total peace.[35]

The doctors discovered Hausheer had Guillain-Barre syndrome, a rare disorder whereby one's immune system attacks their nerves. She spent one month in the intensive care unit regaining her strength and learning how to walk again.

As a result of her NDE, Hausheer says she no longer fears death for herself or others.

CASE #2

In my exploration of NDEs, I also reviewed the work of author Hal Zina Bennett, PhD, who has written more than thirty nonfiction works on shamanism, spirituality, and consciousness. Bennett was introduced to the subject of NDEs when he almost died from a sudden illness at sixteen years old:

> As a boy ... hunting near my home, I [shot a rabbit] ... While skinning the rabbit, I nicked my finger, mingling my own blood with the animal's. ... Within three days I came down with what I thought was the flu, but my fever climbed rapidly, and our family doctor told my parents to rush me to the hospital. My temperature continued to escalate, so I was tucked inside a plastic body bag [that was] packed with ice. Even so, my fever persisted and by the third day I felt totally dissociated from the physical world. ...

> My impression was that I was at least two stories above the hospital roof. I could look down through the structure into the room where my body lay, seeing everything in detail ... but ... felt wide awake and blissfully comfortable. ... I stood at a crossroads, indicated by three paths of light and color. ... To my right was the road to death ... a tunnel. I was certain that once I entered this space, my life back on Earth would be finished. Though I could not see much beyond the tunnel, what I saw was a very different kind of reality, one that I can only describe as formless and invisible but definitely not Nothingness. What I sensed there moved me deeply, excited me, and part of me longed to move into it, if only to satisfy my curiosity. ...

> To my left was a road ... back to life on Earth ... where my body lay. ... I saw my father enter the hospital room, sit down beside my bed and take my hand. He was weeping ... I was either dying or already dead, and was not sure which it was ... I made a decision to reenter my body. ...

> I could no longer see. I could see light and shadow, but no color. ... And even though I felt the impulse to move, my muscles did not respond. I was also having trouble with my speech.

> The doctor ... explained that I had been in a 'mild coma.'... "We thought we were going to lose you for a while. ... You apparently had tularemia," he said, "rabbit fever."

> I later discovered that this was a serious infection ... often fatal. ... I'd lost at least forty pounds in the five or six days I had lain in bed burning with fever. ... My sight returned, and I recovered my ability to move about. But life had changed for me.[36]

As Bennett developed his spiritual interests, he came to see the rabbit differently.

> *I no longer saw it as my foe, but as an almost magical ally and guardian who taught me. ... Through Rabbit, I had come to the beginning of a path that I might never have found. ... Today I wear a small medicine pouch around my neck. Inside, along with other objects, is a small silver figure of a rabbit. ... I must confess, however, that nearly thirty years passed before I could see Rabbit in this positive light and begin integrating what it has shown me and what would become an essential aspect of my personal voice.*[37]

CASE #3

In 1944, Carl Jung had an NDE at the age of sixty-nine, when he almost died from a heart attack. But unlike the previous two cases I have presented, Jung also described having telepathy and precognition *during* his NDE. As Jung writes,

> *In a state of unconsciousness, I experienced deliriums and visions which must have begun when I hung on the edge of death and was being given oxygen and camphor injections. ... I was high up in space. ... I saw the globe of the Earth, bathed in a gloriously blue light. ... I knew that I was on the point of departing from the Earth. ...*
>
> *There was no longer anything I wanted. ... At first the sense of annihilation predominated ... but suddenly that became of no consequence. ...*
>
> *An image floated up. It was my doctor, Dr. H or rather, his likeness—framed by a golden chair or a golden wreath. ... Now he is appearing in ... primal form. Presumably I too was in my primal form. ... As he stood before me, a mute exchange of thought took place between us. Dr. H had been delegated by the Earth to deliver a message ... there was a protest against my going away.*[38]
>
> *Jung also wrote that he felt as if he was "floating in space, in the womb of the universe."*[39]

When first revived, Jung struggled to feel good about being alive. In fact, he was downright angry with his doctor for resuscitating him. Simultaneously, however, he also feared for his physician who had appeared to Jung in his "primal form" during the NDE. Jung tried to warn his doctor that his life was at risk but was unsuccessful. Within days, his doctor died of septicemia. The period following Jung's NDE was an especially productive one. Indeed, Jung wrote many of his most influential works during this time. Jung credited the insights he gained from his NDE with giving him even more courage to explore his ideas and with helping him feel a greater sense of self-acceptance.

PSI ABILITIES WITHIN THE CONTEXT OF NDEs

Although Jung's account is the first I have read, thus far, in which someone has had a precognition *during* their NDE, researchers have found that general psychic ability and psi-related phenomena tend to increase *after* NDEs. Bruce Greyson explains that NDEs may somehow increase an individual's latent sensitivities or may increase a person's awareness of their own paranormal abilities that have always been present but were previously inaccessible.[40]

THE EMOTIONAL TONE OF NDEs

Most people describe positive aftereffects of NDEs and enjoy an increase in spirituality and a decrease in fears of death, but there are some people who do have negative NDEs. Greyson was the first to point out that distressing NDEs can be disturbing and even terrifying.[41] The key difference, according to researchers, involves the general emotional tone of the NDE which leads the person to retain their fear of death.[42] One literature review spanning thirty years of research concluded that as many as one in five NDEs were distressing.[43]

CONTROVERSY OVER MOODY'S FINDINGS

Many have taken issue with Moody's descriptions of NDEs over the years— which is not surprising, given the controversial nature of this topic. Those who oppose Moody's findings tend to assert that neurochemical explanations better account for NDEs. Specifically, researchers taking this position focus on the effects of decreased oxygen, brain damage, shifts in consciousness, hallucinations, the impact of anesthesia and other substances, and the effects of carbon dioxide. Researchers opposing Moody's claims also emphasize how religious beliefs and cultural norms may heavily distort NDE reports.

I have never had an NDE. While I may have wanted to die inside that cold, cavernous studio, Spandex-clad and all alone on audition day, that reprieve from misery never happened. A friend in college did tell me about the night she nearly died in a car accident. In my freshman dorm, we chatted about her life-altering experience. I have to confess, listening to people's concerns as a freshman reminds me of Lucy in *The Peanuts* sitting under a sign that reads:

Psychiatry: 5 cents

My friend said she "levitated" over the crash site and "watched" as the paramedics resuscitated her. Her injuries forced her to miss months of school, but she, thankfully, made a full recovery. I found myself riveted by her story.

Moody also first learned about this topic as a college student. A psychiatrist told him and a group of other students about a time when the psychiatrist "died" for almost nine minutes. At first, Moody "filed it away,"[44] but the story would leave an enormous impression upon him. Tragically, in 1991, Moody had his own NDE after he attempted suicide.

Over the years, millions have been fascinated with Moody's work, and many also have disapproved of his methods. What is not debatable is that Moody started an international discussion about life's ultimate transition. By examining the process of how we die, and through using the lens of formal research questions, Moody provided the first systematic glimpse into our final moments. Since the 1970s, Moody has helped train doctors, nurses, psychologists, hospice workers, and clergy members on the process of grief and dying. His work has brought comfort to millions of people worldwide and has inspired countless researchers.

CHAPTER 9

Curiosity and Skepticism

THE MIND IS ONE OF LIFE'S GREATEST MYSTERIES. PHILOSOPHERS AND scientists alike have tried and failed to fully understand it. Some researchers find such a mystery endlessly intriguing. Others turn away from it, repelled.

There are professionals who discredit anything that is not directly observable. These people tend to be those who believe that "parapsychological events cannot be taken seriously because they are not reproducible in controlled experiments."[1] I imagine that none of these professionals have considered soldiers returning from war.

Surprisingly, the horrors of war do not consistently cause post-traumatic stress disorder (PTSD) in soldiers. According to the US Department of Veterans Affairs and the National Center for PTSD, PTSD is only slightly more common among veterans than among civilians. The numbers may surprise you: at some point in their lives, 7 out of every 100 veterans (or 7 percent) will develop PTSD.[2]

When considering this statistic, it is important to note that a portion of veterans with PTSD remain undiagnosed because they do not actively seek help. Therefore, the actual statistic among US veterans is likely higher than what the government reports. PTSD is also made up of a constellation of different clinical symptoms, and although some people may have certain features of PTSD, they may not meet the full, diagnostic criteria. Thus, this statistic of 7 percent only reflects those who reported their symptoms and those who met the complete diagnostic requirements.

Post-traumatic stress symptoms such as hypervigilance, flashbacks, and repetitive nightmares are some of the worst psychological problems people can endure. Yet, these symptoms do not always appear, to a full-blown degree, among war veterans. Understanding why this happens is difficult. No laboratory on Earth could logistically or ethically replicate the experience of war. Given these facts, would scientists argue that war is not a strong enough emotional trigger to set off intense psychological symptoms? Will they further argue that the 7 percent of war veterans who are diagnosed with PTSD do not actually have this clinical problem because their symptoms, with their respective war origins, could not be reproduced in a laboratory? Of course not. They would also never suggest that war, itself, is not real or that the causality between war and PTSD is not real or that combat PTSD is not a worthy problem to study.

If these scientists truly considered this scenario, they might ask: "Why do 93 percent of veterans not have PTSD, according to the government?" "How are these people different, psychologically, from the other group?" "Can combat PTSD ever fully be studied?" "Could something other than PTSD better explain the veterans' symptoms?" If these professionals raised these questions, we would see their *curiosity* and *skepticism*—the hallmarks of scientists.

Regarding curiosity, The National Academy of Sciences lists "openness" as one of the basic principles that drive researchers in their "Scientific Principles and Research Practices" guidelines.[3] Einstein and Pauli, as we have seen here, embraced this principle when they remained open and curious about spiritual matters. While I don't expect everyone to function at the Nobel laureate level, like these men, I would expect anyone who identifies as a scientist to, at least, meet the minimum standards set forth by the National Academy. Weiss began his work with Catherine with much skepticism and reminded himself repeatedly to keep an open mind and to get more data.[4]

Taking the National Academy of Sciences' guidelines seriously means accepting *the possibility* that the researchers we have reviewed in this book—researchers such as Jung, Rhine, Bem, Stevenson, Tucker, Matlock,

Greyson, Powers et al., and Moody—*might have found something of value* in their parapsychological studies.

Now, let's talk about skepticism, a quality every scientist should lean into and embrace. Skepticism drives researchers to scrutinize and meticulously examine evidence. Skepticism is *not* about reflexively denying whatever is unclear or poorly understood. Discrediting phenomena without first reviewing the facts undermines the foundation of science.

Curiosity and skepticism are at the center of all scientific and academic endeavors. I encourage the reader to examine closely the studies I have presented by exploring the works cited in the Notes sections. Review the research by Bem (2011), Stevenson (1993), and Powers et al., (2017) for instance. Ask whether each of those studies could have been better executed. Consider how the researchers could have boosted the generalizability of their findings. Search for methodological flaws in their research designs. Think of different guiding questions that could have produced stronger results. Assess whether the authors misinterpreted their data. Critical thinking shapes and promotes the scientific process. Disparaging anything immediately is prejudice, not science.

Consider the researchers reviewed in this book: their academic pedigrees are impeccable. Each was driven by curiosity and skepticism throughout their esteemed careers.

Although we may never collect the laurels they did, following their example, we can stay inquisitive. We can examine with an open mind the different topics that come our way, academic or otherwise, regardless of our professions.

What will happen, I wonder, when we embrace this level of openness? When we closely consider new material, and listen past our fears and doubts, what will we discover?

Who will we become?

EPILOGUE

DESPITE HER INITIAL FEARS, CARLA, THE YOUNG DANCER WHO SOUGHT me out, stayed in the dance department and graduated. Soon thereafter, she was hired by a renowned modern dance company. I watched Carla perform with the company years ago at the Joyce Theater in Manhattan. I think I smiled that night for two hours straight.

All four of the owls I handled have passed on. Santiago, the Great Horned, was the last to go, just as she was the lone survivor in her nest as a hatchling. She lived to be thirty-nine. Santiago, Roja, Racho, and Hueco are now part of the Spirit world. Somewhere, they are listening, guiding souls through the beyond.

Qamar remains my psychotherapy client. He has described our work together regarding his father's death as "transformative." We have discussed many other subjects over the years, as well. Throughout this time, he has earned an MBA and recently become engaged to a woman he dearly loves. Currently, he works for a company that serves financially disadvantaged communities. The same values that drove him to give away his scholarship lead him today. Sadly, Qamar lost touch with the student he helped in college. She went back to China during the pandemic, and he fears she may have died from the virus.

The femme-bot at my dream school audition ended up being my favorite instructor in the dance department. Laura was strict but nurturing. She demanded the best out of us, but she did it with kindness, and I greatly respected her for it. The task of turning away hundreds of girls at auditions must have been awful for her. That fearsome femme-bot-thing: it was just a mask.

At the end of my freshman year, my instructors gave me a formal review in a group meeting. I told them that I would be leaving the program to become a psychology major. I could barely look at Laura as I spoke. I was afraid that if I did, I would cry. The task of saying goodbye to her, to my other instructors, and to the field of dance was overwhelming. So, I borrowed Laura's mask.

As a college professor, I have had to fail students over the years. It is a terrible part of the job, but no one can teach ethically without failing folks along the way. What I saw from those students was only a glimpse of their academic trajectories. Their poor grades could never define them.

Each of us, at various points in our life, has been the skater who fell down on the ice but got up over and over again. Each time we fail, we are faced with the choice to get up and try again or to stay down. Who are we when things get tough? Do we get up?

I will never know what would have happened had I not ventured out into the blizzard on that Saturday in 1991. Certainly, my life would have been different.

My Defining Moment gave me a chance to see myself. On that winter day, I saw the girl beneath the leotard and tights and caught a preview of the woman I would become.

Caught in the warp and weft of my failing grades and thriving insecurities lived a straight-A student. But those poor grades needed to come first, because they were essential parts of my life journey.

As a college freshman, I went through what some might call a transformation and found much irony in my experience. By examining myself and making a series of changes, I moved closer toward authenticity.

Jung saw Individuation as a lifelong process. The Self, he believed, is in a continual state of Becoming. While we strive for wholeness, he theorized, we become more connected with ourselves. As with all of us, I am in that never-ending, self-realization process.

I am so thankful my parents forced me to attend college. For it was at that point that my transformation began. But more than anything, I am thankful and proud to have been their daughter. They are with me through all my days, but maybe I will see them again, once more, somewhere in a distant land. Together, we can laugh at my father's jokes. Speak of love and eternity. And dance, in celebration.

GLOSSARY OF PARAPSYCHOLOGICAL TERMS

clairaudience: The extrasensory perception gained from hearing psychic messages.

claircognizance: The extrasensory knowledge gained only through intuition.

clairsentience: The extrasensory awareness gained solely through feeling. One example would be a person feeling a spirit's sadness, rage, physical pain, symptoms of disease, or injury at the time of the apparition's death.

clairvoyance: The extrasensory knowledge of events, people, and objects at various points along the future. This may include visual impressions such as seeing a spirit or seeing a loved one in danger at a future point. Many people who are clairvoyant report seeing images metaphorically. With practice, clairvoyants strengthen their ability to interpret these symbolic images.

extrasensory perception (ESP): Perception that is not gained through the physical senses. This term was coined by Dr. J.B. Rhine.

intermission interval: The mysterious time period in children's reincarnation cases between the previous personality's death and the child's birth. This term was coined by Dr. Ian Stevenson.

mediumship: Also known as the practice of channeling; the ability to communicate with spirits

near-death experience (NDE): The series of profound events that occur while someone is close to dying, often involving the ceasing of brain wave activity or cardiac arrest. This term was coined by Dr. Raymond Moody, Jr.

occult: Comes from the Latin word occultus, meaning hidden; a large category consisting of supernatural beliefs and the paranormal; includes spirituality, astrology, magic spells, tarot cards, and all the various ESP abilities.

paranormal: Denoting events that violate our understanding of time and space and that are not readily explainable by current, mainstream science.

parapsychology: The study of paranormal and psychic phenomena.

precognition: The extrasensory knowledge of a future event.

premonition: A feeling of general forewarning; a vague extrasensory feeling that something ominous will occur.

psychokinesis: The action of moving objects solely with one's mind.

reincarnation: The rebirth of a person or an animal after death, or the belief that one's soul can be reborn into another physical body.

retrocognition: The extrasensory awareness of a past occurrence.

poltergeists: Ghosts that purposefully disrupt specific living and/or working environments by making noises or moving objects.

psi: A large category of psychic abilities not readily explainable by our five standard senses.

psychic: A person who uses multiple psi abilities to understand people, situations, or objects.

psychic medium: A person who has the same psi skills as a psychic, but who can also channel spirits and relay messages from the deceased.

synchronicity: A theory regarding the simultaneous occurrence of events that appear as highly improbable coincidences. This term was coined by Dr. Carl Jung.

telepathy: Mind-to-mind communication; the ability to send and receive thoughts without vocalization.

trance: An altered state of consciousness deliberately induced by a professional intuitive to better access psychic information; usually experienced as pleasant or neutral by the professional.

xenoglossy: A person's ability to speak an unlearned foreign language. This term was coined by Dr. Charles Robert Richet. There are two subsets of xenoglossy:

reactive xenoglossy: The ability exhibited when someone speaks an unknown language in an automatic, rote, non-comprehending manner. This term was coined by Dr. Ian Stevenson.

responsive xenoglossy: A person understands and speaks intelligibly in an unlearned language. This term was coined by Dr. Ian Stevenson.

GLOSSARY OF PSYCHOLOGICAL TERMS

analytical psychology: A school of thought and psychotherapeutic approach developed by Dr. Carl Jung.

anima: Unconscious feminine aspects in a man. This term was coined by Dr. Carl Jung.

animus: Unconscious masculine aspects in a woman. This term was coined by Dr. Carl Jung.

archetypes: Unconscious, universal thought patterns and images believed to be shared with all of humanity; theorized to exist cross-culturally since the beginning of civilization; appear in dreams, myths, religions, fairy tales, legends, art, fantasies, and human behaviors. This term was coined by Dr. Carl Jung.

auditory hallucinations: The sensory perceptions of hearing noises that are not confirmable or measurable by science (examples include voices that command, comment, or criticize a person's behavior).

collective unconscious: A part of the unconscious that is shared with all of humanity; contains a set of knowledge and imagery that people are born with (example: archetypes are theorized to come from the collective unconscious). This term was coined by Dr. Carl Jung.

countertransference: Occurs in psychotherapy when the therapist projects their feelings about important people from their past onto their client. This term was coined by Dr. Sigmund Freud.

déjà vu: Feeling as though one has previously experienced a current situation. There are two subsets of déjà vu:

déjà vecu: Already lived.

déjà visite: Already visited; location based.

dissociation: An unconscious response to anxiety and stress in which a person separates, psychologically, from themselves; may include feeling detached from one's thoughts, feelings, memories, or sense of identity; occurs most commonly as a trauma response.

extraversion: A personality characteristic whereby someone refuels their energy by being around other people. This term was coined by Dr. Carl Jung.

father archetype: Theorized to represent providers, protectors, and wisdom, and is thought to appear in situations concerning individualism, self-determination, challenges, battles, and rules. This term was coined by Dr. Carl Jung.

flashbulb memories: Highly emotionally charged, intense, and spontaneous forms of memory.

flattened affect: Occurs when a person does not express emotion; a symptom that may occur with schizophrenia.

hypervigilance: A state of being highly emotionally alert to the possibility of threats to one's emotional and/or physical safety (commonly seen in trauma).

Individuation: A lifelong psychological process in which someone becomes more of their own, unique person. Dr. Carl Jung introduced this term to the field of psychology.

introversion: A personality characteristic whereby someone refuels their energy by doing activities alone. This term was coined by Dr. Carl Jung.

mandala: Sanskrit word for circle; a Hindu or Buddhist image of a circle that represents the wholeness of the Self according to Dr. Carl Jung.

Myers-Briggs Type Indicator: A psychological test developed by Isabel Myers and Katherine Briggs; based on Dr. Carl Jung's theory of Psychological Types.

persona: A "mask" or an image of oneself that is presented to the outer world. This term was coined by Dr. Carl Jung.

post-traumatic play: Occurs when a child unconsciously repeats traumatic events, symbolically, in their play; represents the child's attempt to understand and process what happened to them; often leaves the child feeling more anxious since the play fails to resolve the matter. This term was coined by Dr. Lenore Terr.

post-traumatic stress disorder (PTSD): A psychological disorder that occurs when a person has difficulty adjusting after a frightening event or series of events; may occur from directly experiencing or witnessing something terrifying; common symptoms include hypervigilance, flashbacks, dissociation, and repetitive nightmares.

quaternity: A four-fold image that is thought to represent wholeness according to Dr. Carl Jung.

recency effect: A memory phenomenon in which items presented last are best remembered.

repression: An unconscious, mental force whereby someone blocks out anxiety-provoking thoughts and feelings. This term was made famous by Dr. Sigmund Freud.

schizophrenia: A psychotic disorder in which a person's thoughts, feelings, and behaviors are severely distorted.

Self: The archetype of wholeness and the product of Individuation according to Dr. Carl Jung.

shadow archetype: That which represents the darkness within the psyche; contains aspects of ourselves that we often try to ignore or deny; (example mentioned in this book: Darth Vader in *Star Wars*). This term was brought to psychology by Dr. Carl Jung.

sublimation: The act by a person of transforming their unacceptable urges such as sex, anger, and aggression into some socially acceptable form. This term was coined by Dr. Sigmund Freud.

thanatology: The scientific study of death and dying.

DARYL BEM, PhD (1938-)

Professor Emeritus, Department of Psychology, Cornell University.

Bem is a social psychologist who is most known for his *self-perception theory* which examines how attitudes are both formed and changed. He has also researched psi extensively as a parapsychologist and focuses on precognition.

Fun Fact: Bem received his BA in physics and began his graduate studies in physics at the Massachusetts Institute of Technology. He left the program and earned his PhD in social psychology at the University of Michigan. Bem calls precognition "the most magical" because of how it violates our understanding of the physical world.

Recommended Reading: If you read only one of Bem's academic papers, make it "Feeling the Future: Experimental Evidence for Anomalous Retroactive Influences on Cognition and Affect."

ALBERT EINSTEIN, PhD (1879–1955)

Einstein is regarded as the most influential physicist of all time. He is best remembered for his *theory of relativity* and his world renowned equation: $E=mc^2$.

Fun Fact: Einstein won the Nobel Prize in Physics in 1921 and was nominated a total of sixty-two times.

Recommended Reading: If you read only one book about this scientist, make it *Einstein* by Walter Isaacson.

SIGMUND FREUD, MD (1856–1939)

The founder of Psychoanalysis and the father of modern psychotherapy began his career in medicine as a neurologist. Freud had a series of patients come to see him with neurological symptoms that could not be explained medically. In the process of trying to help these patients, Freud discovered that their symptoms were psychological in nature. From those early cases, he developed his theories and psychotherapeutic approach.

Freud is most known for his exploration of the unconscious. He created and inspired a wealth of psychological terms—many of which have so greatly affected society that they are still used in our everyday language (e.g., a Freudian slip, whereby someone's "true," unconscious thought unintentionally pops out). In this book, I have covered three Freudian terms—sublimation, repression, and countertransference (see this book's Glossary).

Fun Fact: Freud was nominated for the Nobel Prize on thirty-three occasions (thirty-two times for Physiology or Medicine and once for Literature), but he never won. He was unaware of his multiple nominations, since the list of nominees is announced fifty years after a specific prize is awarded.

Recommended Reading: If you read only one of Freud's books, make it *The Interpretation of Dreams*.

BRUCE GREYSON, MD (1946–)

Professor Emeritus of Psychiatry and Neurobehavioral Sciences at the University of Virginia.

Nearly all of Greyson's research is devoted to near-death experiences (NDEs). He has authored many peer-reviewed journal articles and books on the subject.

Fun Fact: Greyson developed a scale that measures different features of the NDE. His scale has been cited over 450 times by other researchers in their publications.

Recommended Reading: If you read only one of Greyson's books, make it *After: A Doctor Explores What Near-Death Experiences Reveal About Life and Beyond*.

CARL JUNG, MD (1875–1961)

Jung started out as Freud's most famous follower, but when he developed his own school of thought and psychotherapy (Analytical Psychology), he became one of the field's most influential figures in his own right. Jung's notion of the collective unconscious, with its resulting archetypes, is perhaps his greatest contribution to psychology.

I have covered many Jungian terms throughout this book, some in greater depth than others. Examples include: anima, animus, archetypes, collective unconscious, extraversion, Individuation, introversion, mandala, persona, quaternity, Self, and synchronicity (see this book's Glossary).

Fun Fact: Jung was fascinated by art throughout his life and personally created many beautiful works. Examples of his art can be seen in his publication, *The Red Book*.

Recommended Reading: If you read only one of Jung's books, make it *Memories, Dreams and Reflections*.

ELIZABETH KÜBLER-ROSS, MD (1926–2004)

Psychiatrist and author of over twenty books on death and dying, Kübler-Ross is most known for her five-stage model of grief, which includes: denial, anger, bargaining, depression, and acceptance. As a major figure in the development of the hospice system and the "Death with Dignity" movement, Kübler-Ross has greatly helped our culture serve the needs of dying people.

Fun Fact: *Time* magazine listed Kübler-Ross as one of the "100 Most Important Thinkers of the 20th Century."

Recommended Reading: If you read only one of Kübler-Ross's books, make it *On Death and Dying*.

RODERICK MAIN, PhD (?–)

Professor in the Department of Psychosocial and Psychoanalytic Studies, and Director of the Center for Myth Studies, both at the University of Essex.

Main is a highly regarded Jungian scholar who has written many journal articles and books throughout his career. His research and teachings focus largely on Jung's theories concerning religion, mythology, synchronicity, literature, and society.

Fun Fact: Main is currently teaching a course entitled "Dream, Myth, and Magic." I wish I could enroll!

Recommended Reading: If you read only one of Main's books, make it *Jung on Synchronicity and the Paranormal*.

JAMES G. MATLOCK, PhD (1954–)

Research Fellow at the Parapsychology Foundation.

Matlock is an anthropologist who specializes in reincarnation. He has written multiple books and peer-reviewed journal articles on the subject.

Fun Fact: Matlock has worked at both the American Society for Psychical Research in New York City and the Rhine Research Center in Durham, North Carolina.

Recommended Reading: If you read only one of Matlock's books, make it *Signs of Reincarnation: Exploring Beliefs, Cases, and Theory.*

RAYMOND MOODY, JR., MD, PhD (1944–)

As a psychiatrist, philosopher, and author of several books, Moody coined the term near-death experience (NDE). Overall, Moody's work focuses on the afterlife, and he has brought comfort to millions of people worldwide.

Fun Fact: *The New York Times* calls Moody "The Father of the Near-Death Experience" because of his groundbreaking work on the subject.

Recommended Reading: If you read only one of Moody's books, make it *Life After Life.* This book started the entire field of NDE research. To date, it has sold more than thirteen million copies.

WOLFGANG PAULI, PhD (1900–1958)

Pauli was an Austrian theoretical physicist who became one of the pioneers of quantum physics. He is best remembered for discovering the exclusion principle, or Pauli principle, for which he won the Nobel Prize in 1945.

Fun Fact: He also created the term "The Pauli Effect," which describes Pauli's remarkable ability to break experimental laboratory equipment simply by being near it.

Recommended Reading: If you read only one book about this scientist, make it *Pauli and Jung: The Meeting of Two Great Minds* by David Lindorff, PhD.

J.B. RHINE, PhD (1895–1980)

Widely considered the Father of Parapsychology, Rhine pioneered the field at Duke University starting in the 1930s. Rhine coined the term ESP, or extrasensory perception (see this book's Glossary). He was also Jung's first parapsychological colleague.

Fun Fact: The original movie *Ghostbusters* (1984) pokes fun at Rhine's parapsychological studies. In one of the scenes, Bill Murray sits across from subjects while presenting them with Zener cards.

Recommended Reading: If you read only one book about Rhine, make it *J.B. Rhine, Letters 1923–1939: ESP and the Foundations of Parapsychology* Edited by Barbara Ensrud and Sally Rhine Feather.

IAN STEVENSON, MD (1918-2007)

Founder and former Director of the Division of Perceptual Studies at the University of Virginia School of Medicine and Former Chairman of Psychiatry at University of Virginia.

Widely regarded as the world's preeminent past life investigator, Stevenson was known to have researched 3,000 cases of children across the globe who claimed to recall past lives.

Fun Fact: Stevenson told a colleague that he read a list of 3,535 books from 1935–2003 (see Williams' 2022 journal article in the Notes section for Chapter 5: Reincarnation). I wonder what he read!

Recommended Reading: If you read only one of Stevenson's journal articles, make it "Birthmarks and Birth Defects Corresponding to Wounds on Deceased Persons."

JIM B. TUCKER, MD (1960-)

Director of the Division of Perceptual Studies at the University of Virginia and Professor of Psychiatry and Neurobehavioral Sciences at the University of Virginia.

As a child psychiatrist and researcher, Tucker worked alongside Stevenson for several years. He was appointed by Stevenson in 2002 to the position of Director at the Division of Perceptual Studies. Tucker has written books and many peer-reviewed journal articles on reincarnation.

Fun Fact: Tucker quotes Voltaire on his website: "It is not more surprising to be born twice than once; everything in nature is resurrection."

Recommended Reading: If you read only one of Tucker's books, make it *Life Before Life: Children's Memories of Previous Lives.*

BRIAN WEISS, MD (1944-)

Chairman Emeritus of Psychiatry at the Mount Sinai Medical Center in Miami.

Weiss is currently the foremost expert on the past lives of adults. As a psychiatrist, hypnotherapist, and author of several books on the subject, Weiss has been a key figure in past-life regression therapy since the 1980s.

Fun Fact: Therapists and non-professionals alike can study past-life regression directly from Weiss through his five-day training workshops offered by the Weiss Institute.

Recommended Reading: If you read only one of Weiss's books, make it *Many Lives, Many Masters.*

NOTES

CHAPTER 1: THE BIZARRE BEGINNING/ WHAT MAKES A DEFINING MOMENT

1. For more information on Individuation, see Jung, C. G. (Carl Gustav). *The Undiscovered Self.* New York: Penguin Books, 1957.

2. To read McGillivray's complete story, see McGillivray, David. *The Last Pick.* Emmaus, PA: Rodale, Inc, 2006.

3. To study sublimation in greater depth, see Freud, Sigmund. *Leonardo da Vinci and a Memory of His Childhood.* New York: W.W. Norton & Company, 1910.

4. To read the *New York Times* bestselling book on the life of Winston Churchill, see Johnson, Paul. *Churchill.* New York: Penguin Books, 2009.

5. To discover more about Rosa Parks, see Theoharis, Jeanne. *The Rebellious Life of Mrs. Rosa Parks.* Boston: Beacon Press, 2013.

6. Jung, 1957, op cit, 47.

CHAPTER 2: THE BUILDING BLOCKS

1. For more introductory information on parapsychology and its specific terms, see Irwin, Harvey J. and Caroline A. Watt. *An Introduction to Parapsychology. 5th Edition.* Jefferson, NC: McFarland & Company, Inc., 2007.

2. Irwin and Watt, 2007, ob cit.

3. For an excellent glossary of Jungian terms, see Sharp, Daryl. *C.G. Jung Lexicon: A Primer of Terms & Concepts.* Toronto: Inner City Books, 1991.

4. Rachlin, Harvey. "Psychics and Police Work." *Law and Order* 41, no. 9 (1993): 84–88.

5. Wahbeh, Helane and Radin, Dean. "People reporting experiences of mediumship have higher dissociation symptom scores than non-mediums, but below thresholds for pathological dissociation." *F1000 Research 6* (2018): 1416.

6. For a thorough explanation of Jung's theory of synchronicity, see Main, Roderick. *Jung on Synchronicity and the Paranormal.* Princeton: Princeton University Press, 1997.

7. Wahbeh, Helane, Radin, Dean, Yount, G. Woodley Of Menie, M.A., Sarraf M.A. & Karpuj M.V. "Genetics of psychic ability – A Pilot Case-control exome sequencing study." *Explore* 18, no. 3 (2022): 264–271.

8. Wahbeh and Radin, 2018, ob cit.

9. Tsavoussis, Areti, Stawicki, Stanislaw, Stoicea, Nicoleta and Papadimos, Thomas J. "Child-witnessed domestic violence and its adverse effects on brain development: a call for societal self-examination and awareness." *Frontiers in Public Health* 2, (2014): 178.

10. C. G. Jung, Letters. Vol. 1. 1906–1950: Edited by Gerhard Adler in collaboration with Aniela Jaffe. Translation by R.F.C. Hull. Bollingen Series XCV. Princeton, NJ: Princeton University Press, 1973.

11. Main, 1997, ob cit.

12. Main, 1997, ob cit.

13. Mejia, Zameena. "If you have this personality type, chances are you're making more money than your co-workers." CNBC.com. Make it. June 12, 2017. https://www.cnbc.com/2017/06/12/workers-with-this-myers-briggs-personality-type-earns-the-highest-annual-income.html.

14. Rodman, Selden. *Conversations with Artists.* Jenkintown, PA: Capricorn Books, 1961.

15. Herman, William E. and Fair-Schulz, Axel. "The Psychological Odys-

sey of 1909: Car Gustav Jung's Pivotal Encounter with Sigmund Freud During Their Journey to America." *Swiss American Historical Society* 54, no. 2, Article 4. (2018).

16. Sprinthall, R. and Lubetkin, B. "ESP: Motivation as a Factor in Ability." *The Journal of Psychology* 60, (1965): 313–318.

17. Oakley, Colleen. "The Power of Female Intuition: Just what is that sixth sense that sometimes guides you. And what is the best way to tune in?" WebMD. August 10, 2012. https://www.webmd.com/balance/features/power-of-female-intuition.

CHAPTER 3: PRECOGNITIVE DREAMS

1. Bem, D. J. "Feeling the Future: Experimental Evidence for Anomalous Retroactive Influences on Cognition and Affect." *Journal of Personality and Social Psychology* 100, no. 3 (2011): 407–425.

2. Irwin, Harvey J. and Caroline A. Watt. *An Introduction to Parapsychology.* Fifth Edition. Jefferson, NC: McFarland & Company, Inc., 2007.

3. Chalmers, Sarah. "Yes, we do have a sixth sense: The in-depth study of our intriguing dreams that convinced one doctor." Mail Online. October 6, 2009. https://www.dailymail.co.uk/femail/article-1218401/Yes-sixth-sense-The-depth-study-intriguing-dreams-convinced-doctor.html.

4. To learn more about the life of Abraham Lincoln, see the work of his official biographer, Ward Hill Lamon, *Recollections of Abraham Lincoln 1847–1865. Second Edition,* ed. Dorothy Lamon Teillard. (Cambridge: The University Press, 1911), 116–117.

5. Lange, Rense, Schredl, Michael and Houran, James. "What precognitive dreams are made of: The nonlinear dynamics of tolerance of ambiguity, dream recall, and paranormal belief." *Dynamical Psychology: An International, Interdisciplinary Journal of Complex Mental Processes,* January, 2001. https://goertzel.org/dynapsyc/2000/Precog%20Dreams.htm.

6. For more information on Freud's theories and techniques concerning dream analysis, see Freud, Sigmund. *The Interpretation of Dreams.* New York: Oxford University Press Inc., 1899.

7. For Jung's autobiography, see Jung, C.G. (Carl Gustav). *Dreams, Memories and Reflections*. Edited by Aniela Jaffe. Translation by Richard and Clara Winston. New York: Vintage Books, 1963, 361.

8. Jung, 1963, op cit, p. 361.

9. Jung, 1963, op cit.

10. Freud, Sigmund. *The Psychopathology of Everyday Life*. New York: W.W. Norton & Company, 1901, 332–333.

11. Jung, 1963, op cit, p. 303.

12. Jung, 1963, op cit, p. 313.

13. Jung, 1963, op cit.

14. Irwin and Watt, 2007, op cit.

15. Bem, 2011, op cit.

16. Bem, 2011, op cit.

17. Bem, 2011, op cit.

18. Bem, 2011, op cit.

19. Lowery, George. "Study showing that humans have some psychic powers caps Darryl Bem's career.' *Cornell Chronicle*, December 6, 2010. https://news.cornell.edu/stories/2010/12/study-looks-brains-ability-see-future.

20. Irwin and Watt, 2007, op cit.

21. Irwin and Watt, 2007, op cit.

22. Irwin and Watt, 2007, op cit.

23. Irwin and Watt, 2007, op cit.

24. Jung, 1963, op cit.

25. C. G. Jung, *Letters. Vol. 1: 1906–1950*. Edited by Gerhard Adler in collaboration with Aniela Jaffe. Translated by R.F.C. Hull. Bollingen Series XCV. Princeton, NJ: Princeton University Press, 1973.

26. Jung, 1973, op cit.

27. Jung, 1963, op cit, 100.

28. The Editors of Encyclopedia Britannica, "J.B. Rhine," Britannica.com, November 24, 2023. https://www.britannica.com/biography/J-B-Rhine.

CHAPTER 4: OWL MEDICINE

1. All About Birds. "Great Horned Owl." The Cornell Lab, 2024 https://allaboutbirds.org/guide/Great_Horned_Owl.

2. Ogden, Lesley Evans. "The Silent Flight of Owls, Explained." *Audubon*, July 28, 2017. https://www.audubon.org/news/the-silent-flight-owls-explained.

3. Owl Research Institute, https://www.owlresearchinstitute.org.

4. El-Sayed Kitat, Sara. "The Veneration of the Owl in Graeco-Roman Egypt." *International Journal of History and Cultural Studies (IJHCS)* 5, no. 2 (2019): 1–20.

5. El-Sayed Kitat, 2019, op cit.

6. El-Sayed Kitat, 2019, op cit.

7. El-Sayed Kitat, 2019, op cit.

8. Gautier, Achilles. "Animal Mummies and Remains from the Necropolis of Elkab (Upper Egypt)." *Archaeofauna* 14, (2005). 139–170.

9. *Relief Plaque with Face of an Owl Hieroglyph*. Late Period–Ptolemaic Period 400–30B.C., Metropolitan Museum of Art, New York.

10. Muhs, Brian. *The Ancient Egyptian Economy 3000–30 BCE* Cambridge, England: Cambridge University Press, 2016.

11. Greenberg, Mike. "Harpocrates: The God of Silence." *Mythology Source*, April 19, 2021. https://mythologysource.com/harpocrates-god-of-silence.

12. El-Sayed Kitat, 2019, op cit.

13. El-Sayed Kitat, 2019, op cit.

14. Cole, Sara E. "What is the Egyptian Book of the Dead?" Getty. October 19, 2023. https://www.getty.edu/news/what-is-the-egyptian-book-of-the-dead.

15. Hay, Anne. "Owls in Native American Cultures." Buffalo Bill Center of the West. August 6, 2018. https://centerofthewest.org/2018/08/06/owls-native-american-culture.

16. For a more complete review of animal symbolism, see Andrews, Ted. *Animal Speak*. Woodbury, MN: Llewellyn Publications, 2007.

17. El-Sayed Kitat, 2019, op cit.

18. Morris, Desmond. *Owl*. London: Reaktion Books LTD, 2009.

19. Kennesaw State University (2024). https://www.k-state.edu/wwparent/programs/hero/hero-des-owl.htm#:~:text=The%20owl%20is%20the%20bird,was%20the%20guardian%20of%20Acropolis.

20. Newar, Rachel. "Bringing Owls Into the Light." *The New York Times*. April 3, 2017. https://www.nytimes.com/2017/04/03/science/owls-enigma-of-the-owl-mike-unwin-david-tipling.html.

21. El-Sayed Kitat, 2019, op cit.

22. Morris, 2009, op cit.

23. El-Sayed Kitat, 2019, op cit.

24. van Rijn, Rembrandt. *Minerva*. circa 1655, Calouste Gulbenkian Museum, Lisbon.

25. Blasdell, Heather L. "...And There Shall the Lilith Repose." *Mythlore* 14, no. 4 (1988). 4–12.

26. Gaines, Janet H. "Lilith." *Bible Review* 17, no. 5 (2001).

27. Osherow, Michelle. "The Dawn of a New Lilith: Revisionary Mythmaking in Women's Science Fiction." *National Women's Studies Association Journal* 12, no. 1 (2000): 68–83.

28. Patai, Raphael. "Lilith." *The Journal of American Folklore* 77, no 306 (1964): 295–314. (Emphasis made with bold by Brimberg).

29. Blasdell, 1988, op cit, p. 4.

30. Andrews, 2007, op cit.

31. Morris, 2009, op cit.

32. Newar, 2017, op cit.

33. Andrews, 2007, op cit.

34. Todeschi, Kevin. *Edgar Cayce on the Akashic Records*. Virginia Beach, VA: A.R.E. Press, 1998.

35. Andrews, 2007, op cit.

36. Andrews, 2007, op cit.

37. Andrews, 2007, op cit.

38. Morris, 2009, op cit.

39. Funkhouser, Arthur and Perser, Harry R.M. Déjà Vécu and Déjà Visité: Similarities and Differences: Further Results from an Online Questionnaire. *Explore* 14, no. 4 (2018): 277–282.

40. Funkhouser and Perser, 2018, op cit.

41. Andrews, 2007, op cit.

CHAPTER 5: REINCARNATION

1. Kelly, Emily Williams. "Dr. Stevenson's Obituary." University of Virginia School of Medicine. Updated 2015. https://med.virginia.edu/perceptual-studies/wp-content/uploads/sites/360/2015/11/Stevensons-Obit-Emily.pdf.

2. Irwin, Harvey J. and Caroline A. Watt. *An Introduction to Parapsychology*. Fifth Edition. Jefferson, NC: McFarland & Company, Inc., 2007.

3. Tucker, J. "The Case of James Leininger: An American Case of The Reincarnation Type." *Explore*, 12 (2016): 200–207.

4. Pasricha, Satwant K. and Barker, David R. "A case of the reincarnation type in India: The case of Rakesh Gaur." *European Journal of Parapsychology* 3, 1981: 381–408.

5. Irwin and Watt, 2007, op cit.

6. Stevenson, Ian. (1977). "Reincarnation: Field studies and theoretical issues." In *Handbook of Parapsychology*, edited by Benjamin B. Wolman, 631–663. Jefferson, NC: McFarland. 1977.

7. Kelly, 2015, op cit.

8. Stevenson, 1977, op cit.

9. Stevenson, 1977, op cit.

10. Stevenson, 1977, op cit.

11. Wallis, David. "Conversations/Dr. Ian Stevenson; You May be Reading this in Some Future Past Life." *The New York Times*. Sept. 26, 1999.

12. Matlock, James. G. *Signs of Reincarnation. Exploring beliefs, cases and theory*. Lanham, MD: Rowman & Littlefield, 2019.

13. Stevenson, I. "Birthmarks and Birth Defects Corresponding to Wounds on Deceased Persons." *Journal of Scientific Exploration* 7, no. 4 (1993): 403–410.

14. Stevenson, 1993, op cit.

15. Stevenson, 1993, op cit.

16. Stevenson, 1993, op cit.

17. Wallis, 1999, op cit.

18. Stevenson, 1993, op cit.

19. Stevenson, 1993, op cit.

20. Stevenson, 1993, op cit.

21. Shrestha, Rijen, Kanchan, Tanuj and Krishan, Kewal. "Gunshot Wounds Forensic Pathology." *StatPearls*, April 17, 2023. https://ncbi.nlm.nih.gov/books/NBK556119.

22. Stevenson, 1993, op cit.

23. Stevenson, 1993, op cit.

24. Paley, Dror. "Tibial hemimelia: new classification and reconstructive options." *Journal of Child Orthopedics* 10, no. 6 (2016): 529–555.

25. Stevenson, 1993, op cit.

26. Stevenson, 1993, op cit.

27. Tucker, Jim B. "Ian Stevenson and Cases of the Reincarnation Type." *Journal of Scientific Exploration* 22, no.1 (2008): 36–43.

28. Tucker, 2008, op cit.

29. Matlock, 2019, op cit.

30. Matlock, 2019, op cit.

31. Matlock, 2019, op cit.

32. Glanzer, Murray and Cunitz, Anita R. "Two storage mechanisms in free recall." *Journal of Verbal Learning and Verbal Behavior* 5, no. 4 (1966): 351–360.

33. Matlock, 2019, op cit.

34. Matlock, 2019, op cit.

35. Irwin and Watt, 2007, op cit.

36. Matlock, 2019, op cit.

37. Mills, Antonia and Jim B. Tucker, "Reincarnation. Field Studies and Theoretical Issues Today," in *Parapsychology: A Handbook for the 21st Century*, eds. Etzel Cardena, John Palmer & David Marcusson-Clavertz (Jefferson, North Carolina: McFarland & Company, Inc, 2015), 314–326.

38. Mills and Tucker, 2015, op cit.

39. Mills and Tucker, 2015, op cit.

40. Tucker, 2016, op cit.

41. Tucker, 2016, op cit.

42. Tucker, 2016, op cit.

43. *Surviving Death*, Episode 6, "Reincarnation," directed and executive produced by Ricki Stern, 2021, on Netflix, https://www.breakthrufilms.org/survivingdeath.

44. Mills and Tucker, 2015, op cit.

45. Mills and Tucker, 2015, op cit.

46. Stern, 2021, op cit.

47. Stern, 2021, op cit.

48. Matlock, 2019, op cit.

49. Terr, Lenore C. "Forbidden Games: Post-Traumatic Child's Play." *Journal of the American Academy of Child Psychiatry*, 20, 1981: 741–760.

50. Tucker, 2016, op cit.

51. Meaghan O'Leary, PhD (psychic medium) in discussion with the author, February 14, 2023.

52. Weiss, Brian. *Many Lives, Many Masters*. New York: Simon & Schuster, 1988.

53. Zohuri, Bahman. *Physics of Cryogenics*. Amsterdam: Elsevier, 2018.

54. Albert Einstein, personal letter to the family of Michele Besso, March, 1955. Christie's London. https://www.christies.com/features/Einstein-letters-to-Michele-Besso-8422-1.aspx.

CHAPTER 6: SYNCHRONICITY

1. Merriam-Webster. "Synchronicity." 2024. https://www.merriam-webster.com/dictionary/synchronicity.

2. Jung, C. G. (Carl Gustav). *Synchronicity. An Acausal Connecting Principle*. Translation by R.F.C. Hull. Princeton, NJ: Princeton University Press,1960, 31.

3. Main, Roderick. *Jung on Synchronicity and the Paranormal*. Princeton, New Jersey: Princeton University Press. (1997).

4. Main, 1997, op cit, p. 16.

5. Jung, 1960, op cit, p. 19.

6. Main, 1997, op cit.

7. Jung, C.G. (Carl Gustav). *Dreams, Memories and Reflections*. Edited by Aniela Jaffe. Translation by Richard and Clara Winston. New York: Vintage Books, 1963.

8. Jung, 1960, op cit.

9. Jung, 1960, op cit.

10. McDermott, Brett, Forbes, David, Harris, Chris, McCormack, Julie and Gibbon, Peter. "Non-eating disorders psychopathology in children and

adolescents with eating disorders: Implications for malnutrition and symptom severity." *Journal of Psychosomatic Research* 60, no. 3 (2006): 257–261.

11. Bardone-Cone Anna M., Harney, Megan B., Maldonado Christine R., Lawson, Melissa A., Robinson, D. Paul, Smith, Roma and Tosh, Aneesh. "Defining recovery from an eating disorder: Conceptualization, validation, and examination of psychosocial functioning and psychiatric comorbidity." *Behavior Research and Therapy* 48, no. 3 (2010):194–202.

12. Marvanova, Marketa and Gramith, Kirstin. "Role of antidepressants in the treatment of adults with anorexia nervosa." *Mental Health Clinician* 8, no. 3 (2018): 127–137.

13. Jung, C. G. (Carl Gustav). *The Archetypes and the Collective Unconscious. (Collected Works of C.G. Volume 9. Part 1).* Translation by R.F.C. Hull. Princeton, NJ: Princeton University Press, 1959.

14. Lindorff, David. (2004). *Pauli and Jung. The meeting of two great minds.* Wheaton, IL: Quest Books, 2004.

15. Lindorff, 2004, op cit.

16. For readers interested in Jung's "The Personification of The Opposites," see the *Collected Works of C.G. Jung, Volume 14.* Edited and translated by Gerhard Adler and R.F.C. Hull. Princeton, NJ: Princeton University Press, 1970.

17. Main, 1997, op cit.

18. Jung, 1963, op cit, pp. 137–138.

19. Weiss, Brian. *Many Lives, Many Masters.* New York: Simon & Schuster, 1988.

20. Singh, Ashok, K. "Physicochemical, Electronic, and Mechanical Properties of Nanoparticles." *Science Direct,* 2016. https://www.sciencedirect.com/topics/pharmacology-toxicology-and-pharmaceutical-science/pauli-exclusion-principle.

21. Lindorff, 2004, op cit.

22. Halpern, Paul. "The Synchronicity of Wolfgang Pauli and Carl Jung." *Nautilus,* November 18, 2020. https://nautil.us/the-synchronicity-of-wolfgang-pauli-and-carl-jung-238037.

23. Halpern, 2020, op cit.

24. Lindorff, 2004, op cit.

25. Lindorff, 2004, op cit.

26. Jung, 1963, op cit.

27. Lindorff, 2004, op cit.

28. Lindorff, 2004, op cit.

29. Lindorff, 2004, op cit.

30. Schucking, E.L. (1999). "Jordan, Pauli, politics, Brecht ... and a variable gravitational constant." In *On Einstein's Path*, edited by Alex Harvey, 1–14. New York: Springer.

31. Jung, C.G. (Carl Gustav). *The Structure and Dynamics of the Psyche (Collected Works of C.G. Jung Volume 8).* Translated by Gerhard Adler and R.F.C. Hull. Princeton, New Jersey: Princeton University Press, 1975, par. 850.

32. Main, Roderick. "Research on synchronicity: status and prospects." In *Research in Analytical Psychology: Applications from Scientific, Historical, and Cross-Cultural Research*, edited by Joseph Cambray and Leslie Sawin, 135–156. London: Routledge, 2018.

33. 33. Jung, 1963, op cit.

CHAPTER 7: PREMONITION

1. Lamon, Ward Hill. *The Life of Abraham Lincoln.* Coppell, Texas: Jefferson Publication, 1872/2015.

2. Jung, C.G. (Carl Gustav). *Dreams, Memories and Reflections.* Edited by Aniela Jaffe. Translation by Richard and Clara Winston. New York: Vintage Books, 1963.

3. Matlock, James. G. *Signs of Reincarnation. Exploring beliefs, cases and theory.* Lanham, MD: Rowman & Littlefield, 2019.

4. Nobel Prize Organization. "Charles Robert Richet, M.D." Nobelprize. org. January 6, 2024. https://www.nobelprize.org.

5. Weiss, Brian. *Many Lives, Many Masters*. New York: Simon & Schuster, 1988.

6. Matlock, 2019, op cit.

7. Pasricha, Satwant. "Relevance of parapsychology in psychiatric practice." *Indian Journal of Psychiatry* 53, no. 1 (2011): 4–8.

8. Lim, Anastasia, Hoek, Hans W., Deen, Mathijs L. and Blom, Jan.D. "Prevalence and classification of hallucinations in multiple sensory modalities in schizophrenia spectrum disorders." *Schizophrenia Research* 176, *no.* 2–3, (2016):493–499.

9. Thakur, Tanu and Gupta, Vikas. "Auditory Hallucinations." *StatPearls*, February 13, 2023. https://www.ncbi.nlm.nih.gov/books/NBK557633.

10. Powers, Albert R. III., Kelley, Megan S. and Corlett, Philip R. "Varieties of Voice-Hearing: Psychics and the Psychosis Continuum." *Schizophrenia Bulletin* 43, no. 1 (2017): 84–98.

11. Powers et al., 2017, op cit.

12. Powers et al., 2017, op cit.

CHAPTER 8: NEAR-DEATH EXPERIENCES

1. Orlando, Alex. "Can Science Explain Near-Death Experiences?" Mind. *Discover Magazine*, August 23, 2021. https://www.discovermagazine.com/mind/can-science-explain-near-death-experiences.

2. Zingrone, Nancy L., Alvarado, Carlos S., and Hovelmann, Gerd H. "An Overview of Modern Developments in Parapsychology." In *Parapsychology: A Handbook for the 21st Century*, 13–29. Jefferson, NC: McFarland & Company, Inc, 2015.

3. International Association of For Near-Death Studies, Inc., December 8, 2022. http://www.iands.org.

4. Long, Jeffrey. "Near-death experience. Evidence for their reality." *Missouri Medicine* 111, no. 5 (2014): 372–80.

5. van Lommel, P., van Wees, R., Meyers, V. and Elfferich, I. "Near-death experience in survivors of cardiac arrest: A prospective study in the Netherlands." *Lancet* 358, no. 9298 (2001): 2039–45.

6. Hagan, John C. "Near-death experiences—I hope you are comfortable with them by now!" *Missouri Medicine* 112, no. 2 (2015): 88–91.

7. Moody, Raymond. *Life After Life.* New York: Harper Collins Publishers, 1975.

8. Greyson, Bruce. Defining Near-Death Experiences. *Mortality* 4, no. 1 (1999): 7–19.

9. Greyson, 1999, op cit.

10. Moody, 1975, op cit, p. 16.

11. Moody, 1975, op cit, p. 19.

12. Ring, Kenneth. *Life at Death: A scientific investigation of the near-death experience.* New York: Coward, McCann & Geoghegan, 1980.

13. Fenwick, Peter and Elizabeth Fenwick. *The Truth in the Light: An investigation of over 300 near-death experiences.* London: Headline, 1995.

14. Martial, Charlotte, Cassol, Helena, Antonopoulos, Georgios, Charlier, Thomas, Heros, Julien, Donneau, Anne-Francoise, Charland-Verville, Vanessa and Laureys, Steven. "Temporality of Features in Near-Death Experience Narratives." *Frontiers in Human Neuroscience* 11, (2017): 311.

15. Moody, 1975, op cit, p. 20.

16. Moody, 1975, op cit, p. 21.

17. Fenwick and Fenwick, 1995, op cit.

18. Moody, 1975, op cit, pp. 26–37.

19. Martial, et al., 2017, op cit.

20. Weiss, 1988, op cit.

21. Moody, 1975, op cit.

22. Ring, 1980, op cit.

23. Martial, et al., 2017, op cit.

24. Fenwick and Fenwick, 1995, op cit.

25. Martial, et al., 2017, op cit.

26. Weiss, 1988, op cit.

27. Moody, 1975, op cit.

28. Ring, 1980, op cit.

29. Mood, 1975, op cit, pp. 60–61.

30. Moody, 1975, op cit.

31. Moody, 1975, op cit, p. 71.

32. Martial, et al., 2017, op cit.

33. Martial, et al., 2017, op cit.

34. Moody, 1975, op cit, p. 90.

35. Hausheer, Jean Renee. "Getting comfortable with near-death experiences. My unimaginable journey: a physician's near-death experience." *Missouri Medicine* 111, no. 3, (2014):180–183.

36. Bennett, Hal Zina. *Spirit Animals and the Wheel of Life.* Charlottesville, VA: Hampton Roads Publishing Company, Inc., 2000, 28–31.

37. Bennett, 2000, op cit.

38. Jung, 1963, op cit, pp. 289–292.

39. Jung, 1963, op cit, p. 293.

40. Greyson, Bruce. "Increase in Psychic Phenomena Following New-Death Experiences" *Theta* 11, no. 2 (1983): 26–29.

41. Hagan, 2015, op cit.

42. Bush, Nancy Evans and Greyson, Bruce. "Distressing near-death experiences: The basics." *Missouri Medicine* 111, no. 6 (2014): 486–90.

43. Bush and Greyson, 2014, op cit.

44. Moody, 1975, op cit, p. 6.

CHAPTER 9: CURIOSITY AND SKEPTICISM

1. Lindorff, David. *Pauli and Jung. The meeting of two great minds.* Wheaton, IL: Quest Books, 2004, 97.

2. United States Department of Veterans Affairs. "PTSD: National Center for PTSD." US Department of Veterans Affairs, November 30, 2023. http://www.ptsd.va.gov.

3. National Academy of Sciences. Panel on Scientific Responsibility and the Conduct of Research. *Responsible Science. Ensuring the Integrity of the Research Process Volume I.* Washington, D.C.: National Academies Press, 1992.

4. Weiss, Brian. *Many Lives, Many Masters.* New York: Simon & Schuster, 1988.

ACKNOWLEDGEMENTS

WRITING THIS BOOK HAS BEEN A SPECIAL JOURNEY OF ITS OWN. Throughout, several people have helped me bring my thoughts and feelings to paper.

First, I am deeply thankful for my extraordinary editor, Katie Hall for her unwavering guidance and support. She has pushed me, challenged me, and believed in me as a writer.

Thank you also to Amber Qureshi for her astute editorial suggestions on "the first final." I am so fortunate to have worked with her.

I owe much to my first readers—H.J.S. Schielke, PhD; Joel M. Liebowitz, PhD; Amy Liebowitz; Laura Shields; and Meaghan O'Leary, PhD—for their insightful feedback. A special thank you to Dr. Schielke, for our discussions of Defining Moments and Jungian theory, and to Dr. O'Leary, for being interviewed by me.

Thank you to Jason Rabe and Leo Kron, MD, for saving me decades ago. I could not have written any of this without you.

And thank you to Qamar and Matt, and to all my clients whom I can never truly name. Thank you for entrusting me to serve as your psychologist. It is my honor to help you. I am grateful to be a part of your lives.

DAVIS K. BRIMBERG, PhD, TRAINED AT HARVARD UNIVERSITY as a doctoral intern and postdoctoral fellow. She received her doctorate from Yeshiva University. She taught college, graduate, and medical students as an adjunct professor. Dr. Brimberg is a licensed clinical psychologist in private practice. In addition to her clinical and academic work, she served for several years as a volunteer Handler/Educator of owls at a wildlife center. She lives outside of Seattle.

Made in United States
Troutdale, OR
12/04/2024

25924197R00104